I0426512

SOCIAL PROBLEMS AND SOCIAL LEGISLATION (11SWP13)

(SYLLABUS AND STUDY MATERIAL)

PROJECT MSW,

DEPARTMENT OF SOCIAL WORK,

PSG COLLEGE OF ARTS AND SCIENCE, COIMBATORE,

(2012 – 2014 BATCH)

COMPILED BY: T.M.SURESH

CONTENTS COMPILED BY : G.SANTHOSH AND THIVYA VILASHINI

AND ALL MSW STUDENTS

SYLLABUS:

UNIT I:

Concept of social problem-meaning, causes, effect, preventive and remedial measures-individual disorganization, family disorganization and social disorganization-concept of social legislation-meaning, classification, objective-concept of social justice-need and important-concept of social policy-need and importance.

UNIT II:

Problem of women-marriage, dowry, divorce, grounds for divorce, problem of working women-physical and mental harassment – property right to women-maintenance –the Hindu marriage act1958-special marriage act 1954-the Hindu adoption and maintenance act 1956- dowry abolition act 1961-the medical termination of pregnancy act 1971-prevention of immoral traffic act 1956-transgender problems and transgender.

UNIT III:

Problems of children- destitution- physically and mentally challenged children-illiteracy-mallnutrition-maladjustmenting-childhood-child labour- the child prohibition and regulation act 1986-child marriage restraint 1929-the juvenile justice act 2000- prohibition and regulation amendment act 1978.

UNIT IV:

Problems of youth-youth policy and youth problem-problem of aged-causes and effect-problem of SC and ST -untouchablity-the protection of civil rights act 1955-the SC and ST prevention of atrocities act 1989-persones with disability (equal opportunity, protection of civil rights) full protection act 1995.

UNIT V:

Poverty - illiteracy-unemployment-corruption- juvenile delinquency-alcoholism and drug addiction-commercial sex-AIDS-terrorism-environmental pollution.

UNIT I:

Concept of social problem-meaning, causes, effect, preventive and remedial measures-individual disorganization, family disorganization and social disorganization-concept of social legislation-meaning, classification, objective-concept of social justice-need and important-concept of social policy-need and importance.

SOCIAL PROBLEMS

Social problems are the general factors that affect and damage society. A social problem is normally a term used to describe problems with a particular area or group of people in the world. Social problems often involve problems that effect real life. Examples can include:

- Crime
- Sexual transmitted disease
- Anti social behavior
- Poverty
- Drug abuse
- Alcohol abuse
- Economic Deprivation
- Unemployment

These problems occur in almost every area all over the world, but in some areas it tends to happen more frequently, and to a more severe extent.

Examples of areas with high social problems

Middleborough, England.
Middleborough is officially the most deprived and worst place of living in the United Kingdom due to its social problems and factors of life. The town was given this particular position because of its frequent social problems, including: High levels of crime, high levels of unemployment, high levels of urban poverty, high levels of drug abuse and the lowest income on average in the country.

In 2009, Adair County had 137 DUI arrests, 160 liquor law violations, 131 drug arrests and 24 methamphetamine laboratory seizures in 2009 (Behavioral Health Profile for Adair County, 2011, p. 1). The manufacture of methamphetamine has been particularly problematic for rural Missouri. Missouri is the number one state in the country for methamphetamine trafficking. In 2002, one of every six methamphetamine labs confiscated in the United States was Missouri (Gundy, 2006, p. 7). According to the Kirksville Police Department, methamphetamine is their number one crime problem. This high prevalence of methamphetamine abuse leads to 40% of school dropouts in Adair County (Gundy, 2006, p. 7).

Theories on why social problems occur

The main cause of social problems is because of unemployment, which is also a social problem itself. Many industrial towns in England were booming in the mid 20th century because of their shipbuilding and mining industries. When these places were shut down in the 1980's the unemployment rate reached its highest point in English history. The lack of money in these areas attracted other social problems and therefore social and economic development in these areas was stunted

THE CONCEPT OF SOCIAL DIS ORGANISTION

The concept of social disorganization as we shall use it in this and the following volumes refers primarily to institutions and only secondarily to men. Just as group-organization embodied in socially systematized schemes of behavior imposed as rules upon individuals never exactly coincides with individual life-organization consisting in personally systematized schemes of behavior, so social disorganization never exactly corresponds to individual disorganization. Even if we imagined a group lacking all internal differentiation, i. e., a group in which every member would accept all the socially sanctioned and none but the socially sanctioned rules of behavior as schemes of his own conduct, still every member would systematize these schemes differently in his personal evolution, would make a different life-organization out of them, because neither his temperament nor his life-history would be exactly the same as those of other members. As a matter of fact, such a uniform group is a pure fiction; even in the least differentiated groups we find socially sanctioned rules of behavior which explicitly apply only to certain classes of individuals and are not supposed to be used by others in organizing theirconduct, and we find individuals who in organizing their conduct use some personal schemes of their own invention besides the traditionally sanctioned social rules. Moreover, the progress of social differentiation is accompanied by a growth of special institutions, consisting essentially in a systematic organization of a certain number of socially selected schemes for the permanent achievement of certain results. This institutional organization and the life-organization of any of the individuals through whose activity the institution is socially realized partly overlap, but one individual cannot fully realize in his life the whole systematic organization of the institution since the latter always implies the collaboration of many, and on the other hand each individual has many interests which have to be organized outside of this particular institution

There is, of course, a certain reciprocal dependence between social organization and individual life-organization. We shall discuss in Part IV the influence which social organization exercises upon the individual; we shall see in this and in the following volumes how the life-organization of individual members of a group, particularly of leading members, influences social organization. But the nature of this reciprocal influence in each particular case is a problem to be studied, not a dogma to be accepted in advance

These points must be kept in mind if we are to understand the question of social disorganization. We can define the latter briefly as a decrease of the influence of existing social rules of behavior upon individual members of the group. This decrease may present innumerable degrees, ranging from a single break of some particular rule by one individual up to a general decay of all the institutions of the group. Now, social disorganization in this sense has no unequivocal connection whatever with individual disorganization, which consists in a decrease of the individual's ability to organize his whole life for the efficient, progressive and continuous realization of his fundamental interests. An individual who breaks some or even most of the social rules prevailing in his group may indeed do this because he is losing the minimum capacity of life-organization required by social conformism ; but he may also reject the schemes of behavior imposed by his milieu because they hinder him in reaching a more efficient and more comprehensive life-organization. On the other hand also, the social organization of a group may be very permanent and strong in the sense that no opposition is manifested to the existing rules and institutions; and yet, this lack of opposition may be simply the result of the narrowness of the interests of the group-members and may be accompanied by a very rudimentary; mechanical and inefficient life-organization of each member individually. Of course, a strong group organization may be also the product of a conscious moral effort of its members and thus correspond to a very high degree of life-organization of each of them individually. It is therefore impossible to conclude from social as to individual organization or disorganization, or vice versa. In other words, social organization is not coextensive with individual morality, nor does social disorganization correspond to individual demoralization.

Social disorganization is not an exceptional phenomenon limited to certain periods or certain societies; some of it is found always and everywhere, since always and everywhere there are individual cases of breaking social rules, cases which exercise some disorganizing influence on group institutions and, if not counteracted, are apt to multiply and to lead to a complete decay of the latter. But during periods of social stability this continuous incipient disorganization is continuously neu- tralized by such activities of the group as reinforce with the help of social sanctions the power of existing rules. The stability of group institutions is thus simply a dynamic equilibrium of processes of disorganization and reorganization. This equilibrium is disturbed when processes of disorganization can no longer be checked by any attempts to reinforce the existing rules. A period of prevalent disorganization follows, which may lead to a complete dissolution of the group. More usually, however, it is counteracted and stopped before it reaches this limit by a new process of reorganization which in this case does not consist in a mere reinforcement of the decaying organization, but in a production of new schemes of behavior and new institutions better adapted to the changed demands of the group; we call this production of new schemes and institutions social reconstruction. Social reconstruction is possible only because, and in so far as, during the period of social disorganization a part at least of the members of the group have not become individually disorganized, but, on the contrary, have been working toward a new and more efficient personal life-organization and have expressed a part at least of the constructive tendencies implied in their individual activities in an effort to produce new social institutions.

studying the process of social disorganization we must, of course, in accordance with the chief aim of all science, try to explain it causally, i. e., to analyze its concrete complexity into simple facts which could be subordinated to more or less general laws of causally determined becoming. We have seen in our first volume (Methodological Note) that in the field of social reality a causal fact contains three components, i. e., an effect, whether individual or social, always has a composite cause, containing both an individual (subjective) and a social (objective) element. We have called the subjective socio-psychological elements of social reality attitudes and the objective, social elements which impose themselves upon the individual as given and provoke his reaction social values. If we want to explain causally the appearance of an attitude, we must remember that it is never produced by an external influence alone, but by an external influence plus a definite tendency or predisposition, in other words, by a social value acting upon or, more exactly, appealing to some preexisting attitude. If we want to explain causally the appearance of a social value-a scheme of behavior, an institution, a material product-we cannot do it by merely going back to some subjective, psychological phenomenon of "will" or "feeling" or "reflection," but we must take into account as part of the real cause the preexisting objective, social data which in combination with a subjective tendency gave rise to this effect; in other words, we must explain a social value by an attitude acting upon or influenced by some preexisting social value.

As long as we are concerned with disorganization alone, leaving provisionally aside the following process of reconstruction, the phenomenon which we want to explain is evidently the appearance of such attitudes as impair the efficiency of existing rules of behavior and thus lead to the decay of social institutions. Every social rule is the expression of a definite combination of certain attitudes; if instead of these attitudes some others appear, the influence of the rule is disturbed. There may be thus several different ways in which a rule can lose its efficiency, and still more numerous ways in which an institution, which always involves several regulating schemes, can fall into decay. The causal ex- -planation of any particular case of social disorganization demands thus that we find, first of all, what are the particular attitudes whose appearance manifests itself socially in the loss of influence of the existing social rules, and then try to determine the causes of these attitudes. Our tendency should be, of course, to analyze the apparent diversity and complexity of particular social processes into a limited number of more or less general causal facts, and this tendency can be realized in the study of disorganization if we find that the decay of different rules existing in a given society is the objective manifestation of similar attitudes, that, in other words, many given, apparently different phenomena of disorganization can be causally explained in the same way. We cannot reach any laws of social disorganization, i. e., we cannot find causes which always and everywhere produce social disorganization; we can only hope to determine laws of socio-psychological becoming, i. e., find causes which always and everywhere produce certain definite attitudes, and these causes will explain also social disorganization in all those cases in which it will be found that the attitudes produced by them are the real background of social disorganization, that the decay of given rules or institutions is merely the objective, superficial manifestation of the appearance of these attitudes. Our task is the same as that of the physicist or chemist who does not attempt to find laws of the multiform changes which happen in the sensual appearance of our material environment, but searches for laws of the more fundamental and general processes which are supposed to underlie those directly observable changes, and explains the latter causally only in so far as it can be shown that they are the superficial manifestations of certain deeper, causally explicable effects.

In the next section, "Disorganization of the Family," we offer an explicit illustration of our method, analyzing in detail the problems raised by every document and showing the process by which the conclusion is reached. It would be, of course, superfluous for the professional sociologist and tiresome for the amateur reader if we pursued this exposition of the technique of research throughout the whole volume; in the following sections we state therefore only the general conclusions with just enough particular suggestions to make the bearing of the documents quite clear

EXTRA NOTES

Introduction

The problems created by bad, immoral, illegal, and unpleasant activities which harm and hinder the development of individual and society. There are many social problems existing in our society. These problems can be different from each other depending on place religion, caste, creed and so many other factors. Drug addiction, girl trafficking, gender, discrimination neglecting our rich culture and imitation of western cultures blindly, theft, robbery, dacoit, corruption child marriage etc are the examples of social problems.

 No society is free from problems. There are many social problems prevailing in our society. Some people have the habit of smoking alcoholic drinks. Such habits cause depression, damage of different organs of our body and create disturbances in the society. The habits of smoking and alcoholic drinks creates bad environment in the society which leads the other people to try that and involve them in anti social activities.

We should get rid of such social problems while trying to solve such problems first of all we must try and correctly identify the root cause of the problem. To develop civilized society such problems should be eliminated from the root. An individual alone can do very little to prevent such problems. So we should workuntidily. Some social problems which are existing in May society are given below with its major causes and possible solution

Load shedding: a social problem

Load shedding is one of the major social problems prevailing in the present time n the community especially in Nepal. It is the time period when there is absence of electricity. This is not a problem from the past but now a day's electricity has been basic need of people. People cannot perform any word without electricity. No industries can be run without it. Even household work can't be performed without electricity. It has been great importance in this present life. But there is scarce of it. It is not enough to the entire house. It is lack.There is 8/9 hours of load shedding a day. Due to this people are facing a lot of problems. Every problem has its cause and the solutions.

- Causes: Load shedding
- Carelessness of government
- Leakage and stealing of electricity
- Lack of public awareness
- Lack of technical manpower
- Lack of utilization for better purpose
- Illegal connections to electrical wires and poor maintenance.

Solutions: Load shedding

- The leakage and stealing must be checked
- More technical manpower should be generated.
- Electricity based industries should be established.
- Awareness of use and saving of electricity should be made
- The wind energy should be the next way to electricity
- Lack of drinking water: social problems

Nepal is one of the richest counties in resources of water. But the people of hilly and terrain region are facing the problems of drinking water. "Water, water everywhere, but not drop to drink."

There is an acute problem of population growth so, due to this, the water is not enough to all the people, and they are facing the water problems. As people have to fulfill their needs, they are buying water from the private sector by paying money.

Causes:

- Drinking water
- Lack of awareness in the society people
- No conversation of water resources
- No equal distribution of water in urban areas
- No concept of purification of water before drinking
- Deforestation
- Lack of budget for the drinking water project
- Population growth
- Waiting for the abroad investment

Solution:

- Drinking water
- Awareness should be brought among the societypeople.
- Water sources should be conserved
- Arrangement of drinking water in urban areas should be managed.
- The purification of water concept should be taught to the local people.
- Got should fix the budget required for water project
- Forestation

Government should separate its own budget for the project neither of abroad investment

Alcoholism: a social problem

Alcoholism is one of the major social problems existing in the society. People drink the alcoholic drinks with the various causes. This is the bad habit of people. This problem can be solved by the individual by not involving in the problem. Alcoholism can be done but not regular. Drinking alcohol is one Nepaleseculture which needs to be reformed.

Causes: Alcoholism

1. As the culture festival
2. Illiteracy and unemployment
3. In the company with bad friends
4. Due to personal tensions issue and family conflicts
5. Due to high pressure and temper

Solutions: Alcoholism

- The drinking alcohol should be banned.
- Awareness in the people should be taught about its defect.
- Price hike of the drinks or banned to local areas.
- Dare to say " no" to alcoholic drinks
- Employment opportunities should be provided so that they don't have chance to involve in alcoholism.
- Education should be given about the defect of alcohol in the organs.

Neglecting our cultures and imitation of western cultures: a social problem

Neglecting our culture and imitation of western cultures is also kind of problem. The main reason for this problem is media people watch TV cinemas, telefilms etc. in the TV due to this people forget or neglect our culture and go back either western culture, but we cannot blame directly to media. We should be able to take only good things from such media. If we do so, our culture will be promote spending money lavishly for festivals, feasts etc is the social evils in our society, even giving big party in birthday, naming ceremony etc is also defect of this problem

Causes: Neglecting our culture and imitation of western culture.

- Lack of awareness among people
- Lack of information about Nepalese cultures
- Due to adverse effects of TV, serials, movies

Solution: Neglecting our cultures and imitation of western culture

- Awareness should be brought among people
- The information should about our culture should be provided to future generation
- People should able to take only necessary things from media not unnecessary things
- Child labor: a social problem

Child labor is also a great problem in our country which is still prevailing in our society. We can still see in the market the child working in hotels, restaurant. They are not allowed to do the work in any places. The child working in those places are mostly orphans. So to stop this government has established the various organizations for those orphans and needy people. But some are not going in this; they are working in the hotels and homes for little money.

Causes: Child labor

- Poverty
- Illiteracy
- Unemployment
- Orphans and needy children are involved in it
- Carelessness of parents who have

Solutions: Child labor

- The parents should cure their children's
- Orphans and needy children should be admitted only in SOS, paropakar, bal ashram etc.
- The education must be provided free to all
- The children should not be kept in work

Conclusion: social problem

In conclusion if we need to say something about social problems then social problems are the bad immoral unusual undesirableand violent acts of the people in the society which harms the individual and the society directly and indirectly. No society is free from social problems. Every society or community has problems so we must work untidily to remove those problems from the root. Social problems are the community evil. So, such problems should be identified and abolished in item, otherwise it may greatly damage the society and the nation.

The problems given in the project are the problems of my community. There is always load shedding in the society, which harms me and people of my community socially and economically. A lot of money is spender on buying batteries, invertors, candals. Similarly the lack of drinking water is also the major problem of all hilly and terrain region. There comes an hour of water in the tap a week. Through which the life of people have been difficult. Alcoholism is also the problem of my community;I can see the people fighting after drinking alcohol.

SOCIAL LEGISLATION:

Laws that seek to promote the common good, generally by protecting and assisting the weaker members of society, are considered to be social legislation. Such legislation includes laws assisting the unemployed, the infirm, the disabled, and the elderly. The social welfare system consists of hundreds of state and federal programs of two general types. Some programs, including Social Security, Medicare, unemployment insurance, and Workers' Compensation, are called social insurance programs because they are designed to protect citizens against hardship due to old age, unemployment, or injury. Because people receiving benefits from these programs generally have contributed toward their benefits by paying payroll taxes during the years that they worked, these social insurance programs are usually thought of as earned rewards for work. Programs of a second type, often cumulatively called the Welfare System, provide government assistance to those already poor. These social programs have maximum income requirements and include Aid to Families with Dependent Children, the Food Stamp Program, Medicaid, and Supplemental Security Insurance.

Although the United States has had social welfare legislation since colonial times, its nature and extent has changed over the years. For much of U.S. history, Americans preferred to rely on the marketplace to distribute goods and services equitably among the population. In cases where the market clearly failed to provide for categories of people such as widows, orphans, or the elderly, families were expected to take responsibility for the care of their members. When family members lacked the ability to do so, private, religious, or charitable organizations often played that role. Help from the town, county, or local government was rarely provided, and even then only in those cases where the need arose due to conditions beyond the individual's control, such as sickness, old age, mental incapacity, or widowhood.

The Nineteenth Century

For most of the nineteenth century, social problems too large for family members or private charities to handle fell under the jurisdiction of local government, consisting of the town, city, or county rather than the more distant national government. Local government's power to pass social legislation was premised upon the power of the state to restrict individual liberty and property for the common welfare. Later, while local governments remained involved, states began to assume a share of the obligation of caring for some of their citizens. Beginning in the late 1820s, a number of states founded asylums for the insane. A series of investigations by the reformer Dorothea Dix played an important role in bringing the plight of the mentally ill to the attention of state legislatures. Later in the nineteenth century, state and local governments created other specialized institutions for dependent persons, such as homes for the blind or mentally retarded.

While states and local communities had an interest in alleviating suffering in their jurisdictions, the U.S. legal system at this time limited the types of aid that could be offered. Natural-law concepts such as social Darwinism and laissez-faire economics stressed that redistributing wealth from certain citizens in the form of taxes to other citizens in the form of government payments was inherently unfair. For this reason, the Supreme Court held it constitutionally valid for a state or local government to create a poorhouse but held it unconstitutional for a state to provide stipends to its blind or other needy citizens to allow them to live independently outside an institution. Such judicial reasoning discouraged state legislatures from considering many social welfare laws.

One important exception to the nineteenth-century legal system's aversion to income redistribution took the form of government pensions granted to Union Civil War veterans. Between 1880 and 1910, the federal government devoted more than one-fourth of its expenditures to pensions for veterans and their dependents. The most important piece of benefits legislation was the Dependent Pension Act of 1890, which made pensions available to all who had served honorably in the war for ninety days or more.

The Progressive Era

As the United States became more urbanized and industrialized during the nineteenth and early twentieth centuries, it experienced new problems caused by rapid social, economic, and cultural changes. The rise of large cities and large-scale corporate capitalism strained the ability of local communities to deal with ever-increasing numbers of impoverished citizens or those with special needs. Despite changing social circumstances, many Americans continued to espouse the traditional idea that providing public assistance would make recipient groups dependent on the government. As the size of both the immigrant population and the industrial workforce exploded in urban areas, however, a group of reformers known as Progressives began to advocate that government, rather than private charitable organizations, offered the best hope for solving society's problems. (See Progressive Movement.) Progressives lobbied for statutes to make industrial capitalism more humane. For example, the Sheppard-Towner Maternity and Infancy Protection Act of 1921 was revolutionary because it provided federal funds to match state funds for establishing maternal and child health services in each state. Under the act, full and part-time doctors and public health nurses were hired by state and local public-health agencies to train mothers and midwives in prenatal and infant care and postnatal care for new mothers. Congress failed to renew the statute, however, and it expired in 1929.

The New Deal

The period of greatest activity in the realm of social legislation occurred during President Franklin D. Roosevelt's New Deal. The Great Depression, which began when the stock market collapsed in 1929 and continued until the late 1930s, caused widespread poverty and economic hardship. Millions of Americans lost their jobs and businesses failed. There were no effective state or federal programs to assist the many Americans who needed help. An elderly California physician named Dr. Francis E. Townsend gained great fame by proposing a system of old-age pensions to be administered by the federal government. The Roosevelt administration responded to the popular pressure for such a program, and in 1935, Congress passed the Social Security Act, the centerpiece of the U.S. scheme of social welfare.

Before the act's passage and its validation by the Supreme Court, such legislation ensuring the welfare of U.S. citizens would have been considered unconstitutional as an invasion of powers reserved to the states under the Tenth Amendment. However, in Helvering v. Davis (1937) and Steward Machine Co. v. Davis (1937) the Supreme Court held that Congress had the authority to pass the act under its power to tax and spend for the general welfare of the United States. The Court countered the argument that the federal government was intruding into an area of state authority by stating that the Social Security Act was a necessary response to a nationwide problem that could not be solved without national measures.

The Social Security Act's various provisions ultimately included old-age insurance as well as disability and survivors' benefits and Medicare coverage. Under the oldage insurance provisions of the law, pensions were to be paid to workers who reached the age of sixty-five. The necessary funding for these pensions was to be raised through taxes on employers and employees rather than by general public revenues. The size of individual pensions was to reflect the amount of worker contributions so that those with higher wages received higher pensions. While assisting a great many people, the program did not provide coverage to certain groups of workers with the greatest need. These groups included agricultural and domestic workers, many of whom were black.

Title IV of the act created the program known as Aid to Dependent Children (ADC), which provided matching federal money to help states fund mothers' aid programs. In administering the program, states were given wide discretion in determining who was eligible for ADC and how much they received. The result was that one state's benefits might be five or six times the amount of another state's. In 1939, Congress passed legislation making widows with children eligible for social security benefits if their husbands had contributed to the system while working. Thus widows increasingly tended to rely on social security while ADC gradually came to support more divorced, deserted, and never-married mothers. As a result, a certain amount of stigma has attached to ADC, which unlike social security, is limited to those with low incomes.

Post–new Deal Social Legislation

A second period of great legislative activity on the social welfare front occurred between World War II and the end of the 1970s. For example, in 1944, Congress passed the GI Bill of Rights, which offered a comprehensive set of disability, employment, and educational benefits for returning veterans. Under this legislation, half of all U.S. veterans received benefits for further training or higher education. Federal disability insurance was added to the Social Security Act in 1956.

Early in his presidency, Lyndon B. Johnson put forward an ambitious agenda of social legislation termed the Great Society, which proved to be the most important expansion of the federal government in the United States since the Great Depression. Unlike the New Deal, which was a response to economic hard times, Great Society programs were passed during a time of prosperity. During the Johnson years Congress passed three major civil rights acts. The 1964 act forbade job discrimination and the segregation of public accommodations, the 1965 law guaranteed black voting rights, and a third act in 1968 banned housing discrimination.

The best-known part of the Great Society, however, was a large group of initiatives instituted between 1964 and 1967 known as the War on Poverty. The Economic Opportunity Act of 1964 generated a number of new programs, including Volunteers in Service to America (VISTA), which was intended to operate as a domestic version of the Peace Corps and sent middle-class young people on "missions" into poor neighborhoods, and Upward Bound, which assisted poor high-school students entering college. Other programs included free legal services for the poor, Neighborhood Youth Corps, the Job Corps, and Head Start. These programs were designed to fight poverty by providing training and educational opportunities to those who otherwise might not have them. A key element of these programs was the idea of community action, or encouraging the poor to participate in designing and running the programs intended to assist them.

In 1965, Congress also added the Medicare program to the existing provisions of the Social Security Act. This provision provides funds for medical care for the nation's elderly and its benefits are available to anyone over age sixty-five, regardless of need. (In 1964, the Food Stamp Act had begun to provide food vouchers for those with minimal income.) In 1966 the government extended medical benefits to welfare recipients of all ages through the Medicaid program. (See Medicare and Medicaid.) Also during the 1960s, Congress passed legislation to provide significant federal aid to public education. The Elementary and Secondary Education Act of 1965 offered financial assistance to underfunded public school districts throughout the country, while the Higher Education Act of the same year provided aid to needy college and university students.

When compared to most other countries, the extent of social welfare legislation in place in the United States is quite minimal. Nevertheless, such programs have engendered considerable controversy. In the aftermath of the Great Society, few new or significant programs have been implemented. With the election of Ronald Reagan as president in 1980, the federal government began to attempt to cut back on welfare benefits, relying on the theory that the problem of poverty is best addressed by encouraging the growth of private industry and private-sector jobs. In 1996 President Clinton, working together with a Republican Congress, signed into law the Personal Responsibility and Work Opportunity Reconciliation Act, or welfare reform law, which transformed the welfare system by raising recipients' work requirements and limiting the time period during which benefits are available.

SOCIAL JUSTICE

Social justice is justice exercised within a society, particularly as it is applied to and among the various social classes of a society.

A socially just society is one based upon the principles of equality and solidarity; which pedagogy also maintains that a socially just society both understands and values human rights, as well as recognizing the dignity of every human being. The Constitution of the International Labour Organization affirms that "universal and lasting peace can be established only if it is based upon social justice. Furthermore, the Vienna Declaration and Programme of Action treats social justice as a purpose of the human rights education.[

The term and modern concept of "social justice" was coined by Jesuit priest Luigi Taparelli in 1840 based on the teachings of St. Thomas Aquinas and given further exposure in 1848 by Antonio Rosmini-Serbati. The phrase has taken on a very controverted and variable meaning, depending on who is using it. The idea was elaborated by the moral theologian John A. Ryan, who initiated the concept of a living wage. Father Coughlin also used the term in his publications in the 1930s and the 1940s. It is a part of Catholic social teaching, the Protestants' Social Gospel, and is one of the Four Pillars of the Green Party upheld by green parties worldwide. Social justice as a secular concept, distinct from religious teachings, emerged mainly in the late twentieth century, influenced primarily by philosopher John Rawls.[8]

Theories of social justice

Social justice from religious traditions

Judaism

In To Heal a Fractured World: The Ethics of Responsibility, Rabbi Jonathan Sacks states that social justice has a central place in Judaism. One of Judaism's most distinctive and challenging ideas is its ethics of responsibility reflected in the concepts of simcha ("gladness" or "joy"), tzedakah ("the religious obligation to perform charity and philanthropic acts"), chesed ("deeds of kindness"), and tikkun olam ("repairing the world").

Christianity

Catholicism

Catholic social teaching consists of those aspects of Roman Catholic doctrine which relate to matters dealing with the respect of the individual human life. A distinctive feature of the Catholic social doctrine is their concern for the poorest and most vulnerable members of society. Two of the seven key areas] of "Catholic social teaching" are pertinent to social justice:

Life and dignity of the human person: The foundational principle of all "Catholic Social Teaching" is the sanctity of all human life and the inherent dignity of every human person, from conception to natural death. Human life must be valued above all material possessions.

Preferential option for the poor and vulnerable: Catholics believe Jesus taught that on the Day of Judgement God will ask what each person did to help the poor and needy: "Amen, I say to you, whatever you did for one of these least brothers of mine, you did for me."[The Catholic Church believes that through words, prayers and deeds one must show solidarity with, and compassion for, the poor. The moral test of any society is "how it treats its most vulnerable members. The poor have the most urgent moral claim on the conscience of the nation. People are called to look at public policy decisions in terms of how they affect the poor."

Even before it was propounded in the Catholic social doctrine, social justice appeared regularly in the history of the Catholic Church:

The term "social justice" was adopted by the Jesuit HYPERLINK "http://en.wikipedia.org/wiki/Luigi_Taparelli" Luigi Taparelli in the 1840s, based on the work of St. Thomas Aquinas. He wrote extensively in his journal Civiltà Cattolica, engaging both capitalist and socialist theories from a natural law viewpoint. His basic premise was that the rival economic theories, based on subjective Cartesian thinking, undermined the unity of society present in Thomistic HYPERLINK "http://en.wikipedia.org/wiki/Metaphysics" metaphysics; neither the liberal capitalists nor the communists concerned themselves with public moral HYPERLINK "http://en.wikipedia.org/wiki/Philosophy" philosophy.

Pope Leo XIII, who studied under Taparelli, published in 1891 the encyclical HYPERLINK "http://en.wikipedia.org/wiki/Rerum_Novarum" Rerum Novarum (On the Condition of the Working Classes), rejecting both socialism and capitalism, while defending labor unions and private property. He stated that society should be based on cooperation and not class conflict and competition. In this document, Leo set out the Catholic Church's response to the social instability and labor conflict that had arisen in the wake of industrialization and had led to the rise of socialism. The Pope advocated that the role of the State was to promote social justice through the protection of rights, while the Church must speak out on social issues in order to teach correct social principles and ensure class harmony.

The encyclical Quadragesimo Anno (On Reconstruction of the Social Order, literally "in the fortieth year") of 1931 by Pope Pius XI, encourages a living wage, subsidiarity, and advocates that social justice is a personal virtue as well as an attribute of the social order, saying that society can be just only if individuals and institutions are just.

Pope John Paul II added much to the corpus of the Catholic social teaching, penning three encyclicals which would deal with issues such as economics, politics, geo-political situations, ownership of the means of production, private property and the "social mortgage", and private property. The encyclicals of Laborem Exercens, Solicitudo Rei Socialis, and Centesimus Annus are just a small portion of his overall contribution to Catholic social justice. Pope John Paul II was a strong advocate of justice and human rights, and spoke forcefully for the poor. He addresses issues such as the problems that technology can present should it be misused, and admits a fear that the "progress" of the world is not true progress at all, if it should denigrate the value of the human person.

Pope Benedict XVI's encyclical Deus Caritas Est ("God is Love") of 2006 claims that justice is the defining concern of the state and the central concern of politics, and not of the church, which has charity as its central social concern. It said that the laity has the specific responsibility of pursuing social justice in civil society and that the church's active role in social justice should be to inform the debate, using reason and natural law, and also by providing moral and spiritual formation for those involved in politics.

The official Catholic doctrine on social justice can be found in the book Compendium of the Social Doctrine of the Church, published in 2004 and updated in 2006, by the Pontifical Council Iustitia et Pax.

For more information on Catholic's view of Social Justice, read The Catechism of the Catholic Church 1928-1948

Methodism[edit]

From its founding, Methodism was a Christian social justice movement.

Under John Wesley's direction, Methodists became leaders in many social justice issues of the day, including the prison reform and abolitionism movements. Wesley himself was among the first to preach for slaves rights attracting significant opposition.

Today, social justice plays a major role in the United Methodist Church. The Book of Discipline of the United Methodist Church says, "it is a governmental responsibility to provide all citizens with health careThe United Methodist Church also teaches Population control as part of its doctrine.[

Hinduism

Ancient Hindu society was based on equality of all beings. However, to divide labor society divided itself into hundreds of tribes[Jati]. India was governed by people of non-Hindu faiths from the 8th century which caused ruptures in societal fabric. Caste is a word from the Portuguese word "casta" and caste came to define the jatis only 500 years ago. Considerable social engineering occurred during the British rule which impacted the society's self governance. There was some social injustice in which some jatis considered themselves superior to others. The present day jati hierarchy is undergoing changes for variety of reasons including 'social justice',which is a politically popular stance in democratic India. Institutionalized affirmative action has swung the pendulum. The disparity and wide inequalities in social behaviour to some of the jatis led to various reform movements in hinduism for centuries. While legally outlawed, the caste system remains strong in practice, with social and employment opportunities strongly governed by one's caste of birth.

Islam

The Quran contains numerous references to elements of social justice. For example, one of Islam's Five Pillars is Zakāt, or alms-giving. Charity and assistance to the poor – concepts central to social justice – are and have historically been important parts of the Islamic faith.

In Muslim history, Islamic governance has often been associated with social justice. Establishment of social justice was one of the motivating factors of the Abbasid revolt against the Umayyads. The Shi'a believe that the return of the Mahdi will herald in "the messianic age of justice" and the Mahdi along with the Messiah (Jesus) will end plunder, torture, oppression and discrimination

For the Muslim Brotherhood the implementation of social justice would require the rejection of consumerism and communism. The Brotherhood strongly affirmed the right to private property as well as differences in personal wealth due to factors such as hard work. However, the Brotherhood held Muslims had an obligation to assist those Muslims in need. It held that zakat (alms-giving) was not voluntary charity, but rather the poor had the right to assistance from the more fortunate. Most Islamic governments therefore enforce the zakat through taxes.

Though monetary donations are the most practiced way of zakat, Islam is deeply rooted in the tenets of volunteerism and social activism. Areas of one's communities which require assistance and beneficiaries must be a Muslim's foci if need be, rather than strictly her or his personal or superficial wants. For example, the ecological well-being of the planet (i.e.: animal rights, global warming, natural resources degradation); locally, nationally, globally, is a campaign to which every Muslim must adhere. Many Muslims practice this today by ensuring that they produce minimal waste, give to charity what they no longer need, and spend time in prayer and meditation upon the bounties of nature so as to more mindfully approach all that is provided by nature,and ultimately, AllahOther areas of society in need may be the safety and security of minority populations, i.e.: women or persons of color, children, the elderly, the developmentally or physically disabled, animals, et al.[22] Social justice in Islam is a tenet to which every Muslim must corroborate in his or her daily life, and without which would create a void in all their efforts towards attaining true spirituality and a connection with God.

John Rawls

Political philosopher John Rawls draws on the utilitarian insights of Bentham and Mill, the social contract ideas of John Locke, and the categorical imperative ideas of Kant. His first statement of principle was made in A Theory of Justice where he proposed that, "Each person possesses an inviolability founded on justice that even the welfare of society as a whole cannot override. For this reason justice denies that the loss of freedom for some is made right by a greater good shared by others. A deontological proposition that echoes Kant in framing the moral good of justice in absolutist terms. His views are definitively restated in Political Liberalism where society is seen "as a fair system of co-operation over time, from one generation to the next."

All societies have a basic structure of social, economic, and political institutions, both formal and informal. In testing how well these elements fit and work together, Rawls based a key test of legitimacy on the theories of social contract. To determine whether any particular system of collectively enforced social arrangements is legitimate, he argued that one must look for agreement by the people who are subject to it, but not necessarily to an objective notion of justice based on coherent ideological grounding. Obviously, not every citizen can be asked to participate in a poll to determine his or her consent to every proposal in which some degree of coercion is involved, so one has to assume that all citizens are reasonable. Rawls constructed an argument for a two-stage process to determine a citizen's hypothetical agreement:

The citizen agrees to be represented by X for certain purposes, and, to that extent, X holds these powers as a trustee for the citizen.

X agrees that enforcement in a particular social context is legitimate. The citizen, therefore, is bound by this decision because it is the function of the trustee to represent the citizen in this way.

This applies to one person who represents a small group (e.g., the organiser of a social event setting a dress code) as equally as it does to national governments, which are ultimate trustees, holding representative powers for the benefit of all citizens within their territorial boundaries.

Governments that fail to provide for welfare of their citizens according to the principles of justice are not legitimate. To emphasise the general principle that justice should rise from the people and not be dictated by the law-making powers of governments, Rawls asserted that, "There is ... a general presumption against imposing legal and other restrictions on conduct without sufficient reason. But this presumption creates no special priority for any particular liberty." This is support for an unranked set of liberties that reasonable citizens in all states should respect and uphold — to some extent, the list proposed by Rawls matches the normative human rights that have international recognition and direct enforcement in some nation states where the citizens need encouragement to act in a way that fixes a greater degree of equality of outcome.

The basic liberties according to Rawls

Freedom of thought;

Liberty of conscience as it affects social relationships on the grounds of religion, philosophy, and morality;

Political liberties (e.g. representative democratic institutions, freedom of speech and the press, and freedom of assembly);

Freedom of association;

Freedoms necessary for the liberty and integrity of the person (viz: freedom from slavery, freedom of movement and a reasonable degree of freedom to choose one's occupation); and

Rights and liberties covered by the rule of law.

Criticism

The concept of social justice has come under criticism from a variety of perspectives.

Many authors criticize the idea that there exists an objective standard of social justice. Moral relativists deny that there is any kind of objective standard for justice in general. Non-cognitivists, moral skeptics, moral nihilists, and most logical positivists deny the epistemic possibility of objective notions of justice. Cynics (such as Niccolò Machiavelli believe that any ideal of social justice is ultimately a mere justification for the status quo.

Many other people accept some of the basic principles of social justice, such as the idea that all human beings have a basic level of value, but disagree with the elaborate conclusions that may or may not follow from this. One example is the statement by H. G. Wells that all people are "equally entitled to the respect of their fellowmen.

On the other hand, some scholars reject the very idea of social justice as meaningless, religious, self-contradictory, and ideological, believing that to realize any degree of social justice is unfeasible, and that the attempt to do so must destroy all liberty. Perhaps the most complete rejection of the concept of social justice comes from Friedrich Hayek of the Austrian School of economics:

There can be no test by which we can discover what is 'socially unjust' because there is no subject by which such an injustice can be committed, and there are no rules of individual conduct the observance of which in the market order would secure to the individuals and groups the position which as such (as distinguished from the procedure by which it is determined) would appear just to us. [Social justice] does not belong to the category of error but to that of nonsense, like the term 'a moral stone'

Ben O'Neill of the University of New South Wales argues that, for proponents of "social justice"

The notion of "rights" is a mere term of entitlement, indicative of a claim for any possible desirable good, no matter how important or trivial, abstract or tangible, recent or ancient. It is merely an assertion of desire, and a declaration of intention to use the language of rights to acquire said desire. In fact, since the program of social justice inevitably involves claims for government provision of goods, paid for through the efforts of others, the term actually refers to an intention to use force to acquire one's desires. Not to earn desirable goods by rational thought and action, production and voluntary exchange, but to go in there and forcibly take goods from those who can supply them!

Janusz Korwin-Mikke argues simply: "Either 'social justice' has the same meaning as 'justice' – or not. If so – why use the additional word 'social?' We lose time, we destroy trees to obtain paper necessary to print this word. If not, if 'social justice' means something different from 'justice' – then 'something different from justice' is by definition 'injustice'"

Sociologist Carl L. Bankston has argued that a secular, leftist view of social justice entails viewing the redistribution of goods and resources as based on the rights of disadvantaged categories of people, rather than on compassion or national interest. Bankston maintains that this secular version of social justice became widely accepted due to the rise of demand-side economics and to the moral influence of the civil rights movement[29]

Cosmic values

Hunter Lewis' work promoting natural healthcare and sustainable economies advocates for conservation as a key premise in social justice. His manifesto on sustainability ties the continued thriving of human life to real conditions, the environment supporting that life, and associates injustice with the detrimental effects of unintended consequences of human actions. Quoting classical Greek thinkers like Epicurus on the good of pursuing happiness, Hunter also cites ornithologist, naturalist, and philosopher Alexander Skutch in his book Moral Foundations:

The common feature which unites the activities most consistently forbidden by the moral codes of civilized peoples is that by their very nature they cannot be both habitual and enduring, because they tend to destroy the conditions which make them possible

Pope Benedict XVI cites Teilhard de Chardin in a vision of the cosmos as a 'living host' embracing an understanding of ecology that includes mankinds's relationship to fellow men, that pollution affects not just the natural world but interpersonal relations also. Cosmic harmony, justice and peace are closely interrelated:

If you want to cultivate peace, protect creation.

Social justice movements

Social justice is also a concept that is used to describe the movement towards a socially just world, i.e., the Global Justice Movement. In this context, social justice is based on the concepts of human rights and equality, and can be defined as "the way in which human rights are manifested in the everyday lives of people at every level of society".

A number of movements are working to achieve social justice in society. These movements are working towards the realization of a world where all members of a society, regardless of background or procedural justice, have basic human rights and equal access to the benefits of their society.

Interfaith Social Assistance Reform Coalition

The Interfaith Social Justice Reform Coalition (ISARC) is Ontario's largest interfaith organization dedicated to faith-based approaches to public policy reform in the areas of social justice and poverty eradication. ISARC has a shared hope to mobilize, facilitate, and empower diverse faith communities to research, educate and advocate for public policy for the elimination of poverty in Ontario. ISARC's values include human dignity, social equity, mutual responsibility, fiscal fairness, economic equity and environmental sustainability. Since 1986, ISARC has been a leader in mobilizing faith communities to advocate for systemic change in the Province of Ontario, Canada.

Liberation theology

Liberation theologyis a movement in Christian HYPERLINK "http://en.wikipedia.org/wiki/Theology" theology which conveys the teachings of Jesus Christ in terms of a liberation from unjust economic, political, or social conditions. It has been described by proponents as "an interpretation of Christian faith through the poor's suffering, their struggle and hope, and a critique of society and the Catholic faith and Christianity through the eyes of the poor" and by detractors as Christianity perverted by Marxism and Communism.

Although liberation theology has grown into an international and inter-denominational movement, it began as a movement within the Catholic Church in Latin America in the 1950s – 1960s. It arose principally as a moral reaction to the poverty caused by social injustice in that region. It achieved prominence in the 1970s and 1980s. The term was coined by the Peruvian priest, Gustavo Gutiérrez, who wrote one of the movement's most famous books, A Theology of Liberation (1971). According to Sarah Kleeb, "Marx would surely take issue," she writes, "with the appropriation of his works in a religious context...there is no way to reconcile Marx's views of religion with those of Gutierrez, they are simply incompatible. Despite this, in terms of their understanding of the necessity of a just and righteous world, and the nearly inevitable obstructions along such a path, the two have much in common; and, particularly in the first edition of [A Theology of Liberation], the use of Marxian theory is quite evident

Other noted exponents are Leonardo Boff of Brazil, Jon Sobrino of El Salvador, and Juan Luis Segundo of Uruguay.

Social justice in healthcare

Social justice has more recently made its way into the field of bioethics. Discussion involves topics such as affordable access to health care, especially for low income households and families. The discussion also raises questions such as whether society should bear healthcare costs for low income families, and whether the global

marketplace is a good thing to deal with healthcare. Ruth Faden and

Madison Powers of the Johns Hopkins Berman Institute

of Bioethics focus their analysis of social justice on which inequalities matter the most. They develop a social justice theory that answers some of these questions in concrete settings. Social injustices occur when there is a preventable difference in health states among a population of people. These social injustices take on the form of health inequities when negative health states such as malnourishment, and infectious diseases are more prevalent among an impoverished nation. These negative health states can often be prevented by providing social and economic structures such as Primary Healthcare which ensure the general population has equal access to health care services regardless of income level, gender, education or any other stratifying factor. Integrating social justice to health inherently reflects the social determinants of health model without discounting the role of the bio-medical model.

SOCIAL POLICY

SOCIAL POLICY primarily refers to guidelines, principles, legislation and

activities that affect the living conditions conducive to human

welfare. The Department of Social Policy at the London School

of Economics defines social policy as "an interdisciplinary and applied subject concerned with the analysis of societies' responses to social need. It seeks to foster in its students a capacity to understand theory and evidence drawn from a wide range of social science disciplines, including economics, sociology, psychology, geography, history, law, philosophy and political science. Social Policy is focused on those aspects of the economy, society and policy that are necessary to human existence and the means by which they can be provided. These basic human needs include: food and shelter, a sustainable and safe environment, the promotion of health and treatment of the sick, the care and support of those unable to live a fully independent life; and the education and training of individuals to a level that enables them fully to participate in their society". The Malcolm Wiener

Center for Social Policy at Harvard University describes social policy as "public policy and practice in the areas of health care, human services, criminal justice, inequality, education, and labor." Social policy might also be described as actions that affect the well-being of members of a society through shaping the distribution of and access to goods and resources in that society. Social policy often deals with wicked problems.

History of social policy

The earliest example of direct intervention by government in human welfare dates back to Umar ibn al-Khattāb's rule as the second caliph of Islam in the 6th century. He used zakah collections and also other governmental resources to establish pensions, income support, child benefits, and various stipends for people of the non-Muslim community. [5]

In the West, proponents of scientific social planning such as the sociologist Auguste Comte, and social researchers, such as Charles Booth, contributed to the emergence of social policy in the first industrialised countries. Surveys of poverty exposing the brutal conditions in the urban slum conurbations of Victorian Britain supplied the pressure leading to changes such as the reform of the Poor Law and the welfare reforms carried out by the British Liberal Party. Other significant examples in the development of social policy are the Bismarckian welfare state in 19th century Germany, social security policies introduced under the rubric of the New Deal in the United States between 1933 and 1935, and health reforms in Britain following the Beveridge Report of 1942.

Social policy in the 21st century is complex and in each state it is subject to local, national and supranational political influence. For example, membership of the European Union is conditional on member states' adherence to the Social Chapter of European Union law and other international laws.

Types of social policy

Social policy aims to improve human welfare and to meet human needs for education, health, housing and social security. Important areas of social policy are the welfare state, social security, unemployment insurance, environmental policy, pensions, health care, social housing, social care, child protection, social exclusion, education policy, crime and criminal justice.

The term 'social policy' can also refer to policies which govern human behaviour. In the United States, the term 'social policy' may be used to refer to abortion and the regulation of its practice, euthanasia, homosexuality, the rules surrounding issues of marriage, divorce, adoption, the legal status of recreational drugs, and the legal status of prostitution.

In academia

Social Policy is also an academic discipline focusing on the systematic evaluation of societies' responses to social need. It was developed in the early-to-mid part of the 20th century as a complement to social work studies. London School of Economics professor Richard Titmuss is considered to have established Social Policy (or Social

Administration) as an academic subject and many universities offer the subject for **undergraduate** and **postgraduate** study

UNIT II:

Problem of women-marriage, dowry, divorce, grounds for divorce, problem of working women-physical and mental harassment – property right to women-maintenance –the Hindu marriage act1958-special marriage act 1954-the Hindu adoption and maintenance act 1956-dowry abolition act 1961-the medical termination of pregnancy act 1971-prevention of immoral traffic act 1956-transgender problems and transgender.

Problem of women-

- marriage
- dowry
- divorce
- grounds for divorce,
- problem of working women
- physical and mental harassment

Women

The origin of the Indian idea of appropriate female behaviour can be traced to Manu in 200 BC: "by a young girl, by a young woman, or even by an aged one, nothing must be done independent, even in her own house".

India is a multifaceted society where no generalization could apply to the nation's various regional, religious, social and economic groups. Nevertheless certain broad circumstances in which Indian women live affect the way they participate in the economy.A common denominator in their lives is that they are generally confined to home,with restricted mobility, and in seclusion. Other, unwritten, hierarchical practices place further constraints on women.Throughout history, women have generally been restricted to the role of a home-maker; that of a mother and wife. Despite major changes that have occurred in the status of women in some parts of the world in recent decades, norms that restrict women to the home are still powerful in India, defining activities that are deemed appropriate for women. They are, by and large,excluded from political life, which by its very nature takes place in a public forum.

In spite of India's reputation for respecting women, including treating her as a Goddess, history tells us that women werealso ill-treated. There was no equality between men and women. This is true of ancient, medieval and early modern times barring some revolutionary movements such as that of Basaweshwara, the 12thcentury philosopher in Karnataka, who advocated equality, casteless society, status for women, and betterment of the downtrodden.Reform movements in the 19th and 20th centuries led by great social reformers provided boost to women's legal status in India.

Independence of India heralded the introduction of laws relating to women. The Constitution provided equality to men and women and also gave special protection to women to realise their interests effectively. Special laws were enacted to prevent indecent representation of women in the media and sexual harassment in

workplaces. The law also gives women equal rights in the matter of adoption, maternity benefits, equal pay, good working conditions etc.

At the international level, the UN Charter, the Universal Declaration of Human Rights and Convention on Elimination of All Forms of Discrimination against Women (CEDAW) sought to guarantee better legal status to women.

However, certain contentious issues like the Jammu and Kashmir Permanent Resident (Disqualification) Bill 2004 (which deprived a woman of the status of permanent residency of the State if she married an outsider) and the Supreme Court judgment in Christian Community Welfare Council of India (in an appeal over the Judgment of the High Court, Mumbai). The latterhas permitted, under certain circumstances, the arrest of a woman even in the absence of lady police and at any time in the day or night. These instances have once again brought to the forefront the traditional male domination.

FROM WOMEN TO GENDER

The theoretical foundations of development discourse have experienced many changes over the decades. The role of men and women in the development process has received much attention in the last few decades. Although the principle of equality of men and women was recognized as early as in 1945 in the UN Charter andthe UN Declaration of Human Rights of 1948, researchers have pointed out that development planners worked on the assumption that what would benefit one section of society(especially men) would trickle down to the other(women). The new theory argues that a person's role was specified under a patriarchal framework where the scope of gender -masculine or feminine- was limited within the biological understanding of sex (male/female).

GENDER, DEVELOPMENT, WOMEN'S MOVEMENT

The above situation is especially visible in the world of development, and finds its clearest expression in proliferating references to "gender" in local, national and international forums, and activists.One repeatedly hears of gender bias, gender sensitization, gender planning and gender training, to mention just some of the more common examples of its contemporary use.To begin with,discussions were limited to

only "women", rather than about systemic relations of inequality, involving the relations between both men and women.

The task in India then, as everyone seeks to take account of 60years of independence from two centuries of British colonial rule, is to try and face up to this recent slice of history; a history we would like to claim as our very own. What would an assessment of half a century of development thinking and planning look like from the perspective of women?In the 1991 World Bank Report on Gender and Poverty in India, Lynn Bennett announces: "Now, researchers, women's activities, and government departments are reaching a new consensus: women must be seen as economic actors— actors with a particularly important role to play in efforts to reduce poverty". But, the Shramshakti report on self-employed women and women in the informal sector published in 1988 deplored women's extremely vulnerable working conditions across diverse occupations under high levels of discrimination, as well as the range of health hazards women are exposed to on an everyday basis.

If the World Bank report concluded that poor women are clearly more efficient economic actors, with greater managerial and entrepreneurial skills than men, the

Shramshakti report recommended that women require greater access to resources, especially credit and social services. Wider disparities exist among various women's groups culturally and socially. As a result one can perceive as difference in the cognitive, connotative, and consumption patterns of women residing in various spheres of social and economic layers. The victims of exploitation and oppression have been largely women of the third world countries in general and lower sections among them in particular.

CULTURALLY:

- Gender specific specialization (work)
- Cultural definition of appropriate sex roles
- Expectation of role within relationship
- Belief in the inherent superiority of males
- Customs of marriage (Bride price/Dowry)
- Notion of the family as the private sphere and under male control
- Value that give proprietary right over women and girls.

ECONOMICALLY:

Limited access to cash and credit

Limited access to employment in formal and informal sector.

Limited access to education.

As a result of the cultural and economic factors, women face discrimination right from the childhood. It is held that both in childhood and adulthood males are fed first and better. According to one estimate, even as adults women consume approximately 1000 calories less per day than men. The sex ratio in India stood at 933 females per 1000males at the 2001 census and out of the total population, 120million women lived in abject poverty.Lack of healthcare facilities and poverty has been resulting in India accounting for 27%of all maternal deaths world- wide.Death of young girls in India exceeds that of young boys by over 300,000 each year and every 6th infant death is especially due to gender discrimination.

INDIA'S FEMALE POPULATION

At the 2001 census, India had a female population of 496million. India accounts 15% of World's women characterized by vast regional differences and a variety of cultures. But, social discrimination and economic deprivation on the basis of gender is common to all, irrespective of religion, cast, community, and State.

Empowerment of women, gender discrimination,and violence against women, which have become serious subjects of sociological research in contemporary times, was hitherto neglected.While contemporary social changes have exposed women to unprotected socio-economic, cultural and political environment, there are no corresponding protective social systems and institutions of social justice to safeguard their interests.There are many who are sceptical about women's ability to exercise equal rights with men and about their capacity to play equal role with men. But such mechanization of industry and agriculture, enabling women to compete with men successfully.

Innovations in science and technology have removed the disparity between men and women attributed to physical strength alone. Women are able to handle modern appliances which require intelligence and training and not merely physical strength. Thus, India has now several women working as pilots, driving locomotives, buses, tractors and machinery in workshops.Sex as maternal factor in the area of legal rights has practically disappeared. It is not therefore fair to relegate women as a group to an inferior position in society. The Constitution does not regard sex as a permitted classification and prohibits sex as a basis of differential treatment in all areas of legal rights.

Modernity has resulted in a growing flexibility and changes in the gender roles of men and women. The earlier conception that man was the provider of basic necessities for family and women the child bearer and care taker of home, is no longer valid in the changing social structure and economic compulsions.

In spite of the progress made, rural women and those belonging to the Dalit, Tribal, and nomadic communities remain unaffected. So is the case with Muslim women among the minorities. The latter are far from realizing their basic rights. For instance, the low level of political participation of Muslim women in India is not only a consequence of the lack of resources but also the result of the status of Muslim women in the community. Since women in India have little place in the public arena they also express less faith in the political process.

In spite of the UN Charter of Human Rights and the provisions of the Indian Constitution, women continue to be victims of exploitation. The view that the future generation of a family is carried on and preserved by boys-onlyhas degraded the position of women in society. Similarly, it is noticed that majority of the women are lacking in the spirit of rebellion.If careful attention is not paid and major steps are not taken, the situation will become extremely critical.

Therefore, any attempt to assess the status and problem of women in a society should start from the social framework.Social structure, cultural norms, and value systems are crucial determinants of women's role and their position in society. In respect of the status there is a gap between the theoretical possibilities and their actual realization.

HISTORICAL BACKGROUND

It is very important to know the historical background, if we are to make a study of status of women in India. It is not easy to find answers for questions like when did women start losing their status or who was responsible for this situation. The position that women occupied in the medieval and later the colonial period is of utmost importance. Women were never put on high pedestal in the Shastras.

ANCIENT INDIA

It cannot be clearly stated whether equal rights between men and women prevailed or not during the Vedic period. But available sources show that liberal attitudes and practices pertaining to women did exist. Women were actively involved in religious and social matters. They had some freedom to choose their partner in marriage and a widow was permitted to remarry.

As India started taking steps towards civilization, social discrimination increased. Jainism and Buddhism emerged as potent religious reform movements. According to Buddha, women's spiritual capacities were equal to men's. "Buddhism began as a religion that treated women as equal to men in their capacity for personal spiritual development."1 "The universal prejudices against women, who are said to be weak- minded, fickle, treacherous and impure are shared by the Jains and expressed in several passages of the canon and in the form of maxims."

The high status that women enjoyed during early Vedic period gradually started deteriorating in the late Vedic period. Lineage began to be traced in the male line and sons were the sole heirs to family property. As the economic and social status of sons began to rise, the position of women saw a steep decline.

The position of women reached an all-time low during the age of the Dharmashastras. It is during this age that codes of conduct prescribing behaviour norms for women were evolved. This period saw the exclusion of women from both economic and religious sphere. During the period of Dharmashastra, child marriage was encouraged and widow marriage was looked down upon. The birth of girl child was considered as an ill omen and many parents went to the extent of killing the female infants. The practice of Sati became quite wide spread because of the ill treatment meted out to widows.

MEDIEVAL INDIA

The system of Purdah which was prevalent among royal families, nobles and merchant prince classes prior to the advent of Muslims spread to other classes also. During the medieval period, practices such as polygamy, sati, child marriage, ill treatment of widows already prevalent during the Dharmashastra age gained further momentum. The priestly class misinterpreted the sacred texts and created an impression that all these evil practices had religious sanction.

MODERN INDIA

With the advent of the British, the status of women saw many changes. The East India Company (EIC) was mainly a trading company involved in trade in India. To expand their trade network, they started acquiring territories. As they were a trading company, the question of law and order in the acquired territories posed a great challenge before EIC. Therefore, the company acquired the rights to make laws related to the criminal area. For dealing with civil matters, most importantly, dealing with matters which involved the personal laws, the EIC consulted Moulavis and Pundits. At that time, the customs were devised and sustained by male members. Women were not even consulted. Women's wrongs formed the theoretical basis for men's rights or more properly male duties towards moderating women's lust. Women were not given equal matrimonial rights to property, rights to widows to remarriage, adoption and divorce rights.This situation was severely criticized by the colonial authorities. In return, Indian cultural nationalism argued in favour of Indian tradition. Therefore, the 19thcentury is often termed as the century of social reform. The criticism angered the people of India and caused a serious threat to the longevity of colonial rule in India. Hence, the Queen's Proclamation of 1859 declared that British authorities will not interfere in religious matters of the people.

To bring reforms smoothly in India, legislations transforming the family structure were introduced in Princely States without much opposition. Baroda was the first to introduce divorce provision. The Princely state of Mysore enacted the Infant Marriage Prevention Act of 1894. Keeping pace with these princely states, Malabar part of Madras Presidency and Travancore introduced reforms. But the major drawback was that the Princely States could not stop violation of these laws across their borders.

SATI

The first serious challenge for the reformers was the problem of 'widow immolation' or 'Sati', where Hindu widows climbed the funeral pyres of their husbands; an ancient tradition, prevalent in Bengal, Rajasthan and the South Indian kingdom of Vijayanagar. Sati was never a religious obligation, but it was believed that by burning herself on the funeral pyre, a widow sanctified her ancestors and removed the sins of her husband. She was believed to ascend to the heaven on committing Sati.Strong social pressures on the widow and the status of widows among the Hindus were also factors which helped the growth of this custom. Sati was first abolished in Calcutta in 1798; a territory that fell under the British jurisdiction. Raja Ram Mohan Roy fought bravely for abolition of sati and with assistance from Lord William Bentinck, and a ban on sati was imposed in 1829 in the British territories in India.

WIDOW REMARRIAGE

The status of widows in India was deplorable in that they were not allowed participate in any religious and social functions. Their lives were worse than death; one of the reasons as to why many widows opted for Sati. The upper caste widows were most affected by the then prevailing customs. Prohibition against remarriage of widows was strictly observed only amongst upper caste Hindus. Attempts to make laws to facilitate remarriage of widows by the British were vehemently opposed by the conservative Hindus, who held that remarriage of widows "involved guilt and disgrace on earth and exclusion from heaven."

Ishwar Chandra Vidyasagar, who wrote Marriage of Hindu Widows relying heavily on the Shastras, fought for widow remarriage. Reformers like Mahadev Govind Ranade and Dayananda Saraswati also actively participated in the reform movement, resulting in the enactment of the Hindu Widows Remarriage Act XV of 1856. The major drawback of the Act was that it was only applicable to the Hindus. Also, people showed little enthusiasm to implement the provisions of the Act. In Maharashtra, social reformers like Pandit Vishnu Shastri, Sir R.G. Bhandarkar, Agarkar and D.K. Karve have made significant contributions in this regard.

RIGHT TO PROPERTY

There was a lot of ambiguity on the question of the rights of a widow to property which made it difficult for a widow to remarry. Before the 'Hindu Women's Right to

Property Act XVIII of 1937' and the 'Hindu Succession Act XXX of 1956' came into effect, the Dayabhaga and Mitakshara Lawslaid down that a widow could become a successor to her husband's estate in the absence of a son, son's son, son's son's son of the deceased and the estate which she took by succession to her husband was an estate which she held only during her lifetime. At her death, the estate reverted to the nearest living heir of her dead husband.

CHILD MARRIAGE

Another serious problem that women faced was that of child marriage. Small kids and in some cases even infants in the cradle were married off. Early marriage affected the growth and development of the children. Fixing the minimum age of marriage of men and women by law was voiced as early as the mid-19th century by Ishwar Chandra Vidyasagar and Keshab

Chandra Sen. Vidyasagar argued that early marriage was detrimental to the health of women, their efforts, coupled with that of Mahatma Gandhi, resulted in the passing of the Child Marriage Restraint Act, 1929.

FEMALE INFANTICIDE

A girl is considered a burden by parents. Since a girl child would be going to her husband's place upon marriage, the parents did not want to waste their resources on her upbringing. Again the demand for large dowry and the huge wedding expenses caused a lot of hardship to the parents. So, the parents preferred a male child as they would be able to bring in large dowry. These considerations led to the practice of killing the girl child once she was born.

The practice of female infanticide was common among certain castes and tribes in India, especially in the north and north-western states. The custom of infanticide was particularly prominent among communities which found it difficult to find suitable husbands for their daughters and an unmarried daughter wasconsidered a disgrace to the family. The difficulty was exacerbated by the extravagant expenditure which conventions demanded on the occasion of a daughter's marriage.

The earliest efforts to stop female infanticide were made in Kathiawar and Kutch. In 1795, infanticide was declared to be murder by Bengal Regulation XXI. The evil of female infanticide was ended by propaganda and the forceful action on the part of the British Government. Through the efforts of Keshab Chandra Sen, the Native

Marriage Act of 1872 was passed, which abolished early marriages, made polygamy an offence, sanctioned widow remarriages and inter-caste marriages. In 1901, the Government of Baroda passed the Infant Marriage Prevention Act. This Act fixed the minimum age for marriage for girls at 12 and for boys at 16. In 1930 the Sarda Act was passed, to prevent the solemnization of marriages between boys under the age of 18 years and girls under the age 14 years. However, even today, the Act remains merely on paper on account of several factors.

WOMEN AND POLITICAL PARTICIPATION

Indians wanted a nation state after independence in which women had a right to vote. Unlike the British and American women, Indian women did not face great difficulty in securing franchise. Gandhiji stressed on the need for active participation of masses during the freedom movement, including women. He encouraged total participation of women resulting in the emergence of a large number of women freedom fighters.

The Swadeshi movement, the non-Cooperation (1920-22)movement, the Civil Disobedience movement (1930-34) and the Quit India (1942) movement drew large number of women. Such participation helped women to voice the need for women's participation in the legislation process. Annie Besant, Madame Cama and Sarojini Naidu formed the Women's Indian Association.

But, women still constitute a mere 10% of the legislators in the Parliament and State Assemblies. "According to the 1955 International Parliamentary Union Survey, women hold just 11.7% of all seats in Parliament around the world." Success at the Panchayat level based on reservations for women convinced women's organizations that it is the correct time to extend these reservations to the higher levels. It is a different matter that even at the Panchayat level women members face lot of opposition in as much as the male members of the Panchayat do not consider them as equals. Women face opposition from the family members, often resulting in their resigning their membership. Karnataka and West Bengal are good examples where women have exceeded the reserved 33% with 42% and 39% respectively. These examples show that given a chance women can excel in any field. Women just need the necessary support and encouragement.

INFANT MORTALITY

According to a recent report by *Save the Children*, an international NGO, one-fifthsof the world's new born deaths occur in India. According to the report, over four lakhnew-borns die within the first 24 hours every year in India.India also has the highestunder-five mortality with over 2 million children dying before their fifth birthday. About 90% of these deaths are preventable. One-third of all malnourished children live in India and 46% of children under-3 years are underweight. A child's chances of survival vary in different states-the infant mortality rate in Orissa is 96 per 1000 live births in Kerala it is only 14 per 1000. India ranks 171 out of 175 countries in public health spending

PROBLEMS OF WORKING WOMEN

Working women i.e., those who are in paid employment, face problems at the work- place just by virtue of their being women. Social attitude to the role of women lags much behind the law. The attitude which considers women fit for certain jobs and not others,causes prejudice in those who recruit employees. Thus women find employment easily as nurses, doctors, teachers, secretaries or on the assembly- line.Even when well qualified women are available, preference is given to a male candidate of equal qualifications. A gender bias creates an obstacle at the recruitment stage itself. When it comes to remuneration, though the law proclaims equality, it is not always practiced. The inbuilt conviction that women are incapable of handling arduous jobs and are less efficient than men influences the payment of unequal salaries and wages for the same job. A woman could still bear with these problems if she has control over the money she earns. But in most families her salary is handed over to the father, husband or in-laws.

So the basic motive for seeking employment in order to gain economic Independence is nullified in many women's case. Problems of gender bias beset women in the industrial sector when technological advancement results in retrenchment of employees.

Working women are often subject to sexual harassment even while going to work in the over-crowded public transport system.At the work-place, a working woman experiences sexual harassment from colleagues and her higher officers. The latter may often prove difficult to shake off, when the job is very important for the woman.When a woman is praised for her work or promoted on merit, her advancement is often attributed to sexual favours.

The psychological pressure of all this can easily lead to a woman quitting her job. Most of the problems that beset working women are rooted in the social perspective; that men are the bread winners and women are seen as the house-keepers and child bearers. This typecast role model continues to put obstacles for the working women. A fundamental change is required in the attitudes of the employers, policy makers, family members, and public at large.

WOMEN IN THE INFORMAL SECTOR

The *Shramshakti* report on self-employed women and women in the informal sector that published in 1988 was a crucial report on women in the informal sectors of urban and rural India. The report shows that women are extremely vulnerable to working conditions across diverse occupations, suffering high levels of discrimination, as well as a variety of health hazards.

The report demands enlarging the definition of work to encompass all women engaged in production and reproduction and recognizing women as major rather than supplementary wage earners and calls for formulating strategies to enhance women's control over and owner ship of resources.

The report suggests the appointment of a separate LabourCommissioner to ensure the security of employment of women in the informal sector. The Report throws light on the incredible range of tasks that poor women perform, their often greater contribution to household income despite lower wage earnings, their ability to make scarce resources stretch further under deteriorating conditions etc. The report concludes that poor women are clearly more efficient economic actors, with greater

managerial and entrepreneurial skills them men.

MUSLIM WOMENS RIGHTS IN MUSLIM PERSONAL LAW

MARRIAGE

Marriage is an important social institution which helps in creating the basic unit of human society called family. Under Islamic law Marriage (Nikah) is considered as a solemn contract between the spouses. There are three aspects of marriage in Islamic law.

LEGAL: A Muslim marriage is contractual in form because it makes free consent of the parties an essential element for its validity. This is to ensure that the bridge is not getting marred under any kind of compulsion.

SOCIAL: Islamic law gives the woman an important role at home and in the society. The Prophet both by example and precept encouraged the institution of marriage and recognized it as the basis of society.

RELIGIOUS: The Prophet had said "Marriage is my Sunnah and who ever do not follow my Sunnah is not my true-follower"

Marriage is a mechanism of regulating human relations with religious sanctions and therefore termed a sacred covenant. The Prophet was determined to raise the status of women and accordingly attributed legal and religious importance to marriage.

MAHR AND DOWRY

Mahr, sanctioned by Quran, is a sum of money or other property, which the wife is promised at the time of marriage by her husband and to which she is entitled as a matter of right. The Mahr is meant to protect the wife against the arbitrary exercise of the power of the husband to divorce. Fixing of a high dower operates as a healthy check on the husband's capricious exercise of such right, besides being a mark of respect for the wife.

DIVORCE

Islam regards marriage as a religious obligation but not as indissoluble union. If the situation demands, the marriage can be dissolved. Islam has permitted divorce but it lays emphasis on the fact that divorce should be resorted to only in unavoidable circumstances where there is no other alternative. The Prophet has said "of all things permitted divorce is the most hateful in the sight of God". If the husband and wife are unable to live together or even after genuine efforts for reconciliation fail, the marriage could be properly dissolved.

The Holy Quran says:"Divorce may be pronounced twice and then a woman must be retained in humour or allowed to go with kindness. The verse means that a man who has twice given notice of divorce over a period of two months should remember God before giving notice a third time. Then he should either keep the spouse in a spirit of good will or release her, giving her full rights without any injustice. The prescribed methods of divorce have ensured that it is a well-considered planned arrangement and not just a rash step taken in a fit of emotions.

Marriage Dissolution by the wife

Under Islamic law, a man and a woman entering into a contract of marriage may choose certain mutually agreed conditions upon which their marriage is to take place. The agreed conditions would define their future marital rights and obligations in addition to the normal ones under a valid marriage contract. The spouses may, for example agree that the wife under such an agreement shall have the power to divorce herself on behalf of the husband. Such an agreement, which may be conditional or unconditional, amounts to a delegation of his power by the husband to the wife. When it is conditional the wife would be at liberty to declare divorce on behalf of the husband when he commits a breach of the conditions agreed up on, resulting in the dissolution of her marriage ties with the husband. If it is unconditional the wife has an absolute power, as per the terms of agreement to dissolve the marriage!

MAINTENANCE

Maintenance is the money someone gives to a person that they are legally responsible for, in order to pay for their food, clothes and other necessary things. The implied meaning here is that the maintenance is the money given by the husband to maintain his wife and children. Ina valid marriage, it is the liability of the husband to maintain the wife. There is no liability of maintenance in the case of an irregular marriage where the irregularity is due to absence of witnesses at the time of the ceremony. Where the wife refuses to live with the husband due to non-payment of prompt dower, her refusal will be considered valid and her right of maintenance is not affected whether marriage has been consummated or not. Where the wife refuses to live with the husband or return to her house due to some valid reason (his cruelty) the right of maintenance is not affected. We will not go deep into the other aspects connected with maintenance.

INHERITANCE LAW AND RIGHT TO PROPERTY

Till the dawn of Islam, the Arabs excluded females from inheritance completely. Prophet Muhammad emancipated the status of women and restored them their rightful position in the society. "From what is left by parents and those nearest related there is a share for men and a share for women, whether the property is small or large, a determinate share".A Muslim male is obligated to spend part of his inheritance on his wife, children and house, while the female may keep all of it for herself. Financial support for home and family is considered to the solely responsibility of the husband.

HINDU MARRIAGE ACT 1955

WHO IS A HINDU?

- A child legitimate or illegitimate both of whose parents are Hindus.
- Any child one of whose parents are a Hindu and who is brought up a member of a family to which such parents belongs.
- Who converts or reconverts to Hinduism.

Hindu marriage act:

Conditions for a valid Hindu marriage are

- Both the man and women must be Hindus.
- Neither party should have a spouse living at the time of marriage.
- If a person wants to marry while the spouse is living a divorce should be obtained and it is granted by the court on valid grounds and the divorced person may remarry.

PROHIBITED RELATIONSHIP:

The bride and bridegroom should not be within the degrees of prohibited relationship

a. A lineal ascendant. (i.e.) father and daughter, mother and son

b. Wife or husband of lineal ascendant or descendant (i.e.) father in law and the widow daughter in law.

c. Widow of the brother or of a father's brother or of mother's brother or of grandfathers' brother or of grand mothers' brother.

d. Brother & sister; uncle & niece on the nephew.

Under the customary law, certain marriages are valid. In south India marriage b/w the children of the brother & sister and b/w a male and his sisters' daughter are common.

MARRIAGABLE ACT:

- The bridegroom should have completed the age of 21 years and a bride should be the age of 18 yrs at the time of marriage.
- If either party is a lunatic, or an idiot, the marriage is voidable.
- If either the party is suffering from any kind of mental disorder or mental illness / epilepsy the marriage is voidable.

OTHER GROUNCE:

1. The bride being at the time of marriage is pregnant by some other person that the bridegroom is ignorant of it.

2.   If the consent of the either party for the marriage is obtained by force / fraud.

MARRIAGE CEREMONIES:

According to the Hindu Marriage, "SAPTAPADI" is an important ceremony. "SAPTAPADI" means taking 7 steps around the sacred fire. If even before the 7th step both the parties can disperser from the marriage.

SUYAMARIYADHAI & SEERTHIRUTHA MARRIAGE:

The conditions of such marriages are

1.   The marriage should take place in the presence of relations and friends.
2.   Each party to the marriage should declare that he or she takes other as wife or husband.
3.   Each party to the marriage should garland the other or a sign.
4.   The bridegroom should tie a thali around the neck of the bride.

It was in 1967, the Hindu Marriage Madras Amendment Act 1967 was passed & Sec 7 (A) was introduced into the Hindu Marriage Act 1955. This section deals with the suyamariyadhai and seerthirutha marriage.

DIVORCE :

It is the dissolution of the marriage. It puts an end to the relationship of husband and wife. It can be done only by mean of court.

GROUND FOR DIVORCE:

The husband or the wife may petition for divorce under the following conditions.

1.   Extra marital affair with the third person.

2. Renounce the world by entering the religious order / conversion to another religion.
3. Incurable of unsound mind or suffering from incurable leprosy or vulnerable disease in a communicable form.
4. Not been heard for 7 yrs

THE WIFE HAS FOLLOWING ADDITIONAL GROUNDS FOR DIVORCE:

1. That the husband has been guilty of rape.
2. The brides marriage solemnized at the age of 15 yrs
3. There is no cohabitation for 1 yr / upwards.

TIME FOR THE DIVORCE PETITION:

Before the expiry of 1 yr from the date of marriage.

PROCEEDINGS TO BE IN CAMERA:

Proceedings for divorce and other proceedings under this act shall be conducted in camera. The public will be excluded run the court as the party's may have to wash their dirty linen in the court. The proceedings cannot be printed /published except with the previous permission of the court. Any violation of this is punishable with the fine extending to Rs 1000.

DUTY OF THE COURT:

1. The court should bring about the reconciliation b/w the parties.
2. It should provide for the maintenance and education of the minor children.
3. It may direct monthly payments to be made for the maintenance of the petitioner.

REGISTERATION OF MARRIAGE:

For the purpose of facilitation, proof of Hindu Marriages, provision for registering may be made by the state govt. under this Act. The particulars relating to the marriage may be entered in the marriage register maintained under the rules made by the state govt. But omission to register the marriage does not affect the validity of Hindu Marriage. However register of marriage would give certain advantages since a registration certificate is normally considered by immigrant authorities,

passport authorities as valid proof of marriage.

SPECIAL MARRIAGE ACT 1954:

Any 2 persons irrespective of their religion can marry under the Special Marriage Act 1954 and the inter caste can be registered under this act.

CONDITIONS FOR MARRIAGE :

1. Neither the party should have a husband / wife living at the time of marriage.
2. Neither party is an idiot or lunatic.
3. The bridegroom must have completed the age of 21 yrs and the bride age of 18 yr
4. Both the parties are not within the degree of prohibition relationship.
5. At the time of marriage both the party should be the citizen of the territory to which the Act applies.

NOTICE:

The formalities for a civil marriage under this act began with the notice given by the bride and the bridegroom to the marriage officer of the district immediately before the notice for at least 30 days.

MARRIAGE NOTICE BOOK AND PUBLICATION:

The marriage officer records the notice of the marriage in the marriage notice book and affixes & copy in this office and sends a copy to the marriage officer of that district. This is open to the public & can be inspected without the fee.

OBJECTION:

1. This public notice is an announcement of the marriage and an indication for the objection of any.

2. When the notice is published by the marriage officer, 30 days time is given for any person to raise any objections.

3. From the date of receipt of the objections within 30 days, the marriage officer should enquire into the objections. If he uphold the objections either the party may prefer and appeal to the district court whose decisions shall be final.

4. When there is no objection, both the parties with 3 witness sign in the presence of a marriage officer & the officer declare that they are unmarried and not related within the prohibited relationship and have completed the marriage age.

CERTIFICATE OF MARRIAGE:

The certificate of the marriage officer is the evidence of the marriage under this act.

THE SPECIAL MARRIAGE ACT, 1954

(Act No.43 of 1954)[9th October 1954]

An Act to provide a special form of marriage in certain cases, for the registration of such and certain other marriages and for divorce.

Be it enacted by Parliament in the Fifth Year of the Republic of India as follows:

1. Short title, extent and commencement- (1) This Act may be called the Special Marriage Act, 1954.

(2) It extends to the whole of India except the State of Jammu and Kashmir, and applies also to citizens of India domiciled in the territories to which the Act extends who are in the State of Jammu and Kashmir.

(3) It shall come into force on such date, i.e.1st January, 1955 as the Central Government may, by notification in the Official Gazette, appoint.

2. Definitions- In this Act, unless the context otherwise, requires,-

(a)(* * * *) Omitted

(b)"degrees of prohibited relationship" - a man and any of the persons mentioned in Part I of the First Schedule and a woman and any of the persons mentioned in Part II of the said Schedules are within the degrees of prohibited relationship.

Explanation I.- Relationship includes,-

a)relationship by half or uterine blood as well as by full blood:

b)illegitimate blood relationship as well as legitimate;

c)relationship by adoption as well as by blood;

and all terms of relationship in this Act shall be construed accordingly.

Explanation II.- "Full blood" and "half blood"- two persons are said to be related to each other by full blood when they are descended from a common ancestor by the same wife and by half blood when they are descended from a common ancestor but by different wives.

Explanation III.- "Uterine blood"- two persons are said to be related to each other by uterine blood when they are descended from a common ancestress but by different husbands.

Explanation IV.-In Explns. II and III. "ancestor" includes the father and "ancestress" the mother;

(d)"district", in relation to a Marriage Officer, means the area for which he is appointed as such under sub-section (1) or sub-section (2) of Sec.3;

(e)"District Court" means, in any area for which there is a City Civil Court, and in any other area, the principal Civil Court of original jurisdiction, and includes any other Civil Court which may be specified by the State

Government by notification in the Official Gazette as having jurisdiction in respect of the matters dealt with in this Act:

(f)"prescribed" means prescribed by rules made under this Act;

(g)"State Government", in relation to a Union territory, means the Administrator thereof.

Solemnization of Special Marriages

4. Conditions relating to solemnization of special marriage.-

Notwithstanding anything contained in any other law for the time being in force relating to the solemnization of marriages, a marriage between any two persons may be solemnized under this Act, if at the time of the marriage the following conditions are fulfilled namely:

(a)Neither party has a spouse living:

(b)neither party-

(i)is incapable of giving a valid consent to it in consequence of unsoundness of mind, or

(ii)though capable of giving a valid consent, has been suffering from mental disorder of such a kind or to such an extent as to be unfit for marriage and the procreation of children; or

(iii)has been subject to recurrent attacks of insanity or epilepsy;

(c)the male has completed the age of twenty-one years and the female the age of eighteen years;

(d)the parties are not within the degrees of prohibited relationship:

Provided that where a custom governing at least one of the parties permits of a marriage between them, such marriage may be solemnized, notwithstanding that they are within the degrees of prohibited relationship: and

(e) where the marriage is solemnized in the State of Jammu and Kashmir, both parties are citizens of India domiciled in the territories to which this Act extends.

Explanation- In this section, "customs, in relation to a person belonging to any tribe, community, group or family, means any rule which the State Government may, by notification in the Official Gazette, specify in this behalf as applicable to members of that tribe, community, group or family:

Provided that no such notification shall be issued in relation to the members of any tribes, community, group or family, unless the State Government is satisfied-

(i)that such rule has been continuously and uniformly observed for a long time among those members;

(ii)that such rule is certain and not unreasonable or opposed to public policy; and

(iii)that such rule is applicable only to a family, has not been discontinued by the family.

5.Notices of intended marriage.- When a marriage is intended to be solemnized under this Act, the parties of the marriage shall give notice thereof in writing in the Form specified in the Second Schedule to the Marriage Officer of the district in which at least one of the parties to the marriage has resided for a period of not less than thirty days immediately preceding the date on which such notice is given.

6.Marriage Notice Book and publication.-(1) The Marriage Officer shall keep all notices given under Sec. 5 with the records of his office and shall also forthwith enter a true copy of every such notice in a book prescribed for that purpose, to be called the Marriage Notice Book, and such book shall be open for inspection at all reasonable times, without fee, by any person desirous of inspecting the same.

(2) The Marriage Officer shall cause every such notice to be published by affixing a copy thereof to some conspicuous place in his office.

(3) Where either of the parties to an intended marriage is not permanently residing within the local limits of the district of the Marriage Officer to whom the notice has been given under Sec. 5, the Marriage Officer shall also cause a copy of such notice to be transmitted to the Marriage Officer of the district within whose limits such party is permanently residing, and that Marriage Officer shall thereupon cause a copy thereof to be affixed to some conspicuous place in his office.

7. Objection to marriage.- (1) Any person may, before the expiration of thirty days from the date on which any such notice has been published under sub-section (2) of Sec. 6, object to the marriage on the ground that it would contravene one or more of the conditions specified in Sec.4.

(2)After the expiration of thirty days from the date on which notice of an intended marriage has been published under sub-section (2) of Sec. 6, the marriage may be solemnized, unless it has been previously objected to under sub-section (1).

(3) The nature of the objection shall be recorded in writing by the Marriage Officer in the Marriage Notice Book, be read over and explained if necessary, to the person making the objection and shall be signed by him or on his behalf.

8. Procedure on receipt of objection.- If an objection is made under Sec. 7 to an intended marriage the Marriage Officer shall not solemnize the marriage until he has inquired into the matter of the objection and is satisfied that it ought not to prevent the solemnization of the marriage or the objection is withdraw by the person making it; but the Marriage Officer shall not take more than thirty days from the date of the objection for the purpose of inquiring into the matter of the objection and arriving at a decision.

(2) If the Marriage Officer upholds the objection and refuses to solemnize the marriage, either party to the intended marriage may, within a period of thirty days from the date of such refusal, prefer an appeal to the District Court within the local limits of whose jurisdiction the Marriage Officer has his office, and the decision of the District Court on such appeal shall be final, and the Marriage Officer shall act in conformity with the decision of the Court.

9. Powers of Marriage Officers in respect of inquiries.- (1)For the purpose of any inquiry under Sec.8, the Marriage Officer shall have all the powers vested in a Civil Court under the Code of Civil Procedure, 1908(5 of 1908), when trying a suit in respect of the following matters, namely:

(a)summoning and enforcing the attendance of witnesses and examining them on oath;

(b)discovery and inspection;

(c)compelling the production of documents;

(d)reception of evidence on affidavits; and

(e)issuing commissions for the examination of witnesses;and any proceeding before the Marriage Officer shall be deemed to be a judicial proceeding within the meaning of Sec.193 of the Indian Penal Code(45 of 1960).

2) If it appears to the Marriage Officer that the objection made to an intended marriage is not reasonable and has not been made in good faith he may impose on the person objecting costs, by way of compensation not exceeding one thousand rupees, and award the whole, or any part thereof to the parties to the intended marriage, and any order of costs so made

may be executed in the same manner as a decree passed by the District Court within the local limits of whose jurisdiction the Marriage Officer has his office.

10. Procedure on receipt of objection by Marriage Officer abroad.-

Where an objection is made under Sec.7 to a Marriage Officer in the State of Jammu and Kashmir

in respect of an intended marriage in the State and the Marriage Officer, after making such inquiry into the matter as he thinks fit, entertains a doubt in respect thereof, he shall not solemnize the marriage but shall transmit the record with such statement respecting the matter as he thinks fit to the Central Government, and the Central Government, after making such inquiry into the matter and after obtaining such advice as it thinks fit, shall give its decision thereon in writing to the Marriage Officer shall act in conformity with the decision of the Central Government.

11.Declaration by parties and witnesses.- Before the marriage is solemnized the parties and three witnesses shall, in the presence of the Marriage Officer, sign a declaration in the Form specified in the Third Schedule to this Act, and the declaration shall be countersigned by the Marriage Officer.

12.Place and form of solemnization.- (1) The marriage may be solemnized at the office of the Marriage Officer or at such other place within a reasonable distance therefrom as the parties may desire, and upon such conditions and the payments of such additional fees as may be prescribed.

2) The marriage may be solemnized in any form which the parties may choose to adopt:

Provided that it shall not be complete and binding on the parties unless each party says to the other in the presence of the Marriage Officer and the three witnessess and in any language understood by the parties,- "I (A) take thee (B), to be my lawful wife (or husband)".

13. Certificate of marriage.-(1) When the marriage has been solemnized the Marriage Officer shall enter a certificate thereof in the Form specified in the Fourth Schedule in a book to be kept by him for that purpose and to be called the Marriage Certificate Book and such certificate shall be signed by the parties to the marriage and the three witnesses.

(2) On a certificate being entered in the Marriage Certificate Book by the Marriage Officer, the certificate shall be deemed to be conclusive evidence of the fact that a marriage under this Act has been solemnized and that all formalities respecting the signatures of witnesses have been complied with.

14. New notice when marriage not solemnized within three months.- Whenever a marriage is not solemnized within three calender months from the date on which notice thereof has been given to the Marriage Officer as required by Sec. 5 or where an appeal has been filed under sub- section (2) of Sec.8, within three months from the date of the decision of the District Court on such appeal or where the record of a case has been transmitted to the Central Government under Sec.10, within three months from the date of decision of the Central Government, the notice and all other proceedings arising therefrom shall be deemed to have lapsed, and no marriage Officer shall solemnize the marriage until a new notice has been given in the manner laid down in this Act.

CHAPTER III

Registration of Marriage Celebrated in other forms

15. Registration of marriages celebrated in other forms.-

Any marriage celebrated, whether before or after the commencement of this Act, other than a marriage solemnized under the Special Marriage Act, 1872 or under this Act, may be registered under this Chapter by a Marriage

Officer in the territories to which this Act extends if the following conditions are fulfilled, namely:

(a)a ceremony of marriage has been performed between the parties and they have been living together as husband and wife ever since

(b)neither party has at the time of registration more than one spouse living;

(c)neither party is an idiot or a lunatic at the time of registration:

(d)the parties have completed the age of twenty-one year at the time of registration;

(e)the parties are not within the degrees of prohibited relationship:

Provided that in case of a marriage celebrated before the commencement of this Act, this condition shall be subject to any law, custom or usage having the force of law governing each of them which permits of a marriage between the two; and

(f) the parties have been residing within the district of the Marriage Officer for a period of not less than thirty days immediately preceding the date on which the application is made to him for registration of the marriage.

16.Procedure for registration.- Upon receipt of an application signed by both the parties to the marriage for the registration of their under this chapter, the Marriage Officer shall give public notice thereof in such manner as may be prescribed and after allowing a period of thirty days for objection and after hearing any objection received within that period, shall, if satisfied that all the conditions mentioned in Sec. 15 are fulfilled, enter a certificate of the marriage in the Marriage Certificate Book in the Form specified in the Fifth Schedule and such certificate shall be signed by the parties to the marriage and by three witnesses.

17.Appeals from orders under Sec. 16.- Any person aggrieved by any order of a Marriage Officer refusing to register a marriage under this Chapter may, within thirty days from the date of order, appeal against that order to the

District Court within the local limits of whose jurisdiction the Marriage Officer has his office, and the decision of the District Court on such appeal shall be final, and the Marriage Officer to whom the application was made shall act in conformity with such decision.

18.Effect of registration of marriage under this Chapter.-

Subject to the provisions contained in sub-section (2) of Sec.24 where a certificate of marriage has been finally entered in the Marriage Certificate Book under this Chapter, the marriage shall, as from the date of such entry, be deemed to be a marriage solemnized under this Act, and all children born after the date of the ceremony of marriage (whose names shall also be entered in the Marriage Certificate Book) shall in all respects be deemed to be and always to have been the legitimate children of their parents:

Provided that nothing contained in this section shall be construed as conferring upon any such children any rights in or to the property of any person other than their parents in any case where, but for the passing of this Act, such children would have been incapable of possessing or acquiring any such rights by reason of their not being the legitimate children of their parents.

CHAPTER IV

Consequences of Marriage under this Act

19.Effect of marriage on member of undivided family- The marriage solemnized under this Act of any member of an undivided family who professes the Hindu, Buddhist, Sikh or Jaina religion shall be deemed to effect his severance from such family.

20.Rights and disabilities not affected by Act.- Subject to the provisions of Sec. 19, any person whose marriage is solemnized under this Act, shall have the same rights and shall be subject to the same disabilities in regard to the right of succession to any property as a person to whom the Caste Disabilities Removal Act, 1850 (21 of 1850), applies.

21.Succession to property of parties married under Act.-
Notwithstanding any restrictions contained in the Indian Succession
Act,1925 (39 of 1925), with respect to its application to members of certain
communities, succession to the property of any

person whose marriage is solemnized under this Act and to the property of
the issue of such marriage shall be regulated by the provisions of the said
Act and for the purposes of this section that Act shall have effect as if
Chapter III of Part V (Special Rules for Parsi Intestates) had been omitted
therefrom.

21-A. Special provision in certain cases .- Where the marriage is
solemnized under this Act of any person who professes the Hindu,
Buddhist, Sikh or Jain religion with a person who professes the Hindu,
Buddhish, Sikh or Jain religion. Secs. 19 and 21 shall not apply and so much
of Sec. 20 as creates a disability shall also not apply.

CHAPTER V

Restitution of Conjugal Rights and Judicial Separation

22. Restitution of conjugal rights.- When either the husband or the wife
has, without reasonable excuse, withdrawn from the society of the other
the aggrieved party may apply by petition to the District Court for
restitution of conjugal rights, and the Court, on being satisfied of the truth
of the statements made in such petition, and that there is no legal ground
why the application should not be granted, may decree restitution of
conjugal rights accordingly.

Explanation- Where a question arises whether there has been reasonable
excuse for withdrawal from the society, the burden of proving reasonable
excuse shall be on the person who has withdrawn from the society.

23. Judicial separation.-(1) A Petition for judicial separation may be presented to the District Court either by the husband or the wife.-

(a)on any of the grounds specified in sub-section (1) and sub-section (1-A) of Sec. 27 on which a petition for divorce might have been presented;or

(b)on the grounds of failure to comply with a decree for restitution of conjugal rights and the Court, on being satisfied of the truth of the statements made in such petition, and that there is no legal ground why the application should not be granted, may decree judicial separation accordingly.

(2) Where the Court grants a decree for judicial separation, it shall be no longer obligatory for the petitioner to cohabit with the respondent, but the Court may, on the application by petition of either party and on being satisfied of the truth of the statements made in such petition rescind the decree if it considers it just and reasonable to do so.

CHAPTER VI

Nullity of Marriage and Divorce

24. Void marriages.- (1) Any marriage solemnized under this Act shall be null and void (and may, on a petition presented by either party thereto against the other party, be so declared) by a decree of nullity if-

(i)any of the conditions specified in Cls.(a),(b), (c) and (d) of Sec. 4 has not been fulfilled : or

(ii)the respondent was impotent at the time of the marriage and at the time of the institution of the suit.

(2) Nothing contained in this section shall apply to any marriage deemed to be solemnized under the Act within the meaning of Sec. 18, but the registration of any such marriage under Chapter III may be declared to be of no effect if the registration was in contravention of any of the conditions specified in Cls.(a) to (e) of Sec. 15:

Provided that no such declaration shall be made in any case where an appeal has been preferred under Sec.17 and the decision of the District Court has become final.

25. Voidable marriages.- Any marriage solemnized under this Act shall be voidable and may be annulled by a decree of nullity, if-

(i)the marriage has not been consummated owing to the wilful refusal of the respondent to consummate the marriage ;or

(ii)the respondent was at the time of the marriage pregnant by some person other than the petitioner; or

(iii)the consent of either party to the marriage was obtained by coercion or fraud, as defined in the Indian Contract Act, 1872 (9 of 1872):

Provided that in the case specified in Cl.(ii) the Court shall not grant a decree unless it is satisfied-

(a)that the petitioner was at the time of the marriage ignorant of the facts alleged;

(b)that proceedings were instituted within a year from the date of the marriage; and

(c)the marital intercourse with the consent of the petitioner has not taken place since the discovery by the petitioner of existence of the grounds a decree :

Provided further that in the case specified in Cl.(iii), the Court shall not grant a decree if,-

(a)proceedings have not been instituted within one year after the coercion had ceased or, as the case may be, the fraud had been discovered; or (b)the petitioner has with his or her free consent lived with the other party to the marriage as husband and wife after the coercion had ceased or as the case may be, the fraud had been discovered.

26. Legitimacy of children of void and voidable marriages.-

(1)Notwithstanding that a marriage is null and void under Sec. 24, any child of such marriage who would have been legitimate if the marriage had been valid, shall be legitimate, whether such child is born before or after the commencement of the Marriage Laws(Amendment) Act, 1976, and whether or not a decree of nullity is granted in respect of that marriage under this Act and whether or not the marriage is held to be void otherwise than on a petition under this Act.

(2)Where a decree of nullity is granted in respect of a voidable marriage under Sec.25, any child begotten or conceived before the decree is made, who would have been the legitimate child of the parties to the marriage if at the date of the decree it has been dissolved instead of being annulled, shall be deemed to be their legitimate child notwithstanding the decree of nullity.

(3)Nothing contained in sub-section (1) or sub-section (2) shall be construed as conferring upon any child of a marriage which is null and void or which is annulled by a decree of nullity under Sec. 25, any rights in or to the property of any person, other than the parents, in any case, where, but for the passing of this Act, such child would have been incapable of possessing or requiring any such rights by reason of his not being the legitimate child of his parents.

27. Divorce.-(1) Subject to the provisions of this Act and to the rules made thereunder, a petition for divorce may be presented to the District Court either by the husband or the wife on the ground that the respondent-

(a)has, after the solemnization of the marriage had voluntary sexual intercourse with any person other than his or her spouse; or (b)has deserted the petitioner for a continuous period of not less than two years immediately proceeding the presentation of the petition; or

(c)is undergoing a sentence of imprisonment for seven years or more for an offence as defined in the Indian Penal Code (45 of 1860); or

(d)has since the solemnization of the marriage treated the petitioner with cruelty; or

(e)has been incurably of unsound mind, or has been suffering continuously or intermittently from mental disorder of such a kind, and to such an extent that the petitioner cannot reasonably be expected to live with the respondent.

Explanation- In this Clause-

(a)the expression "mental disorder" means mental illness, arrested or incomplete development of mind, psychopathic disorder or any other disorder or disability of mind and includes schizophrenia;

(b)the expression "psychopathic disorder" means a persistent disorder or disability of mind (whether or not including sub-normality of intelligence) which results in abnormally aggressive or seriously irresponsible conduct on the part of the respondent and whether or not it requires or is susceptible to medical treatment; or

(f) has been suffering from venereal disease in a communicable form; or

(g) has been suffering from leprosy, the disease not having been contracted from the petitioner; or

(h) has not been heard of as being alive for a period of seven years or more by those persons who would naturally have heard of the respondent if the respondent had been alive;

Explanation- In this sub-section, the expression "desertion" means desertion of the petitioner by the other party to the marriage without reasonable cause and without the consent or against the wish of such party and includes the wilful neglect of the petitioner by the other party to the marriage, and its grammatical variations and cognate expressions shall be construed accordingly.

(1-A) A wife may also present a petitioner for divorce to the District Court on the ground.-

(i)that her husband has, since the solemnization of the marriage, been guilty of rape, sodomy or bestiality;

(ii)that in a suit under Sec. 18 of the Hindus Adoptions and Maintenance Act, 1956 (78 of 1956), or in a proceeding under Sec. 125 of the Code of Criminal Procedure, 1973 (2 of 1974), or under the corresponding Sec. 488 of the Code of Criminal Procedure, 1898 (5 of 1898), a decree or order, as the case may be, has been passed against the husband awarding maintenance to the wife notwithstanding that she was living apart and that since the passing of such decree or order, cohabitation between the parties has not been resumed for one year or upwards.

(2) Subject to the provisions of the Act and to the Rules made thereunder, either party to a marriage, whether solemnized before or after the commencement of the Special Marriage (Amendment) Act, 1970, may present a petition for divorce to the District Court on the ground-

(i)that there has been no resumption of cohabitation as between the parties to the marriage for a period of one year or upwards after the passing of a decree for judicial separation in a proceeding to which they were parties; or

(ii)that there has been no restitution of conjugal rights as between the parties to the marriage for a period of one year or upwards after the passing of a decree for restitution of conjugal rights in a proceeding to which they were parties.

27-A. Alternate relief in divorce proceedings- In any proceeding under this Act, on a petition for a dissolution of marriage by a decree of divorce, except in so far as the petition is founded on the ground mentioned in Cl. (h) of sub-section (1) of Sec. 27, the Court may, if it considers it just so to do, having regard to the circumstances of the case, pass instead a decree for judicial

separation.

28. Divorce by mutual consent.-(1) Subject to the provisions of this Act and to the rules made thereunder, a petition for divorce may be presented to the District Court by both the parties together on the ground that they have been living separately for a period of one year or more, that they have not been able to live together and that they have mutually agreed that the marriage should be dissolved.

(2) On the motion of both the parties made not earlier than six months after the date of the presentation of the petition referred to in sub-section (1) and not later than eighteen months after the said date, if the petition is not withdrawn in the meantime, the District Court shall, on being satisfied, after hearing the parties and after making such inquiry as it thinks fit, that a marriage has been solemnized under this Act and that the avertments in the petition are true, pass a decree declaring the marriage to be dissolved with effect from the date of the decree.

29. Restriction on petitions for divorce during first three years after marriage.-(1) No petition for divorce shall be presented to the District Court unless at the date of the presentation of the petition one year has passed since the date of entering the certificate of marriage in the Marriage Certificate Book:

Provided that the District Court may, upon application being made to it allow a petition to be presented before one year has passed on the ground that the case is one of exceptional hardship suffered by the petitioner or of exceptional depravity on the part of the respondent, but if it appears to the

District Court at the hearing of the Petition that the petitioner obtained leave to present the petition by any misrepresentation or concealment of the nature of the case, the District Court may, if it pronounces a decree, do so subject to the condition that the decree shall not have effect until after the expiry of one year from the date of the marriage or may dismiss the petition, without prejudice to any petition, which may be brought after the expiration of the said one year upon the same or substantially the same facts, as those proved in support of the petition so dismissed.

(2) In disposing of any application under this section for leave to present a petition for divorce before the expiration of one year from the date of the marriage, the District Court shall have regard to the interests of any children of the marriage, and to the question whether there is a reasonable probability of a reconciliation between the parties before the expiration of the said one year.

30. Re-marriage of divorced persons- Where a marriage has been dissolved by a decree of divorce, and either there is no right of appeal against the decree or if there is such a right of appeal, the time for appealing has expired without an appeal having been presented or an appeal has been presented but has been dismissed, either party to the marriage may marry again.

CHAPTER VII

Jurisdiction and Procedure

31. Court to which petition should be made.- (1) Every petition under Chapter V or Chapter VI shall be presented to the District Court within the local limits of whose original civil jurisdiction-

(i) the marriage was solemnized; or

(ii)the respondent, at the time of the presentation of the petition resides; or (iii)the parties to the marriage last resided together; or

(iv)the petitioner is residing at the time of the presentation of the petition, in a case where the respondent is, at that time, residing outside the territories to which this Act extends or has not been heard of as being alive for a period of seven years by those who would naturally have

heard of him if he was alive.

(2) Without prejudice to any jurisdiction exercisable by the Court under sub-section (1), the District Court may, by virtue of this sub-section, entertain a petition by a wife domiciled in the territories to which this Act extends for nullity of marriage or for divorce if she is resident in the said territories and has been ordinarily resident , therein for a period of three years immediately preceding the presentation of the petition and the husband is not resident in the said territories.

32. Contents and verification of petitions.- (1) Every petition under Chapter V or Chapter VI shall state, as distinctly as the nature of the case permits, the facts on which the claim to relief is founded and shall also state that there is no collusion between the petitioner and the other party to the marriage.

(2) The statements contained in every such petition shall be verified by the petitioner or some other competent person in the manner required by law for the verification of plaints and may, at the hearing, be referred to as evidence.

33. Proceedings to be in camera and may not be printed or published.- (1) Every proceeding under this Act shall be conducted in camera and it shall not be lawful for any person to print or publish any matter in relation to any such proceeding except a judgment of the High Court or of the Supreme Court printed or published with the previous permission of the Court.

(2) If any person prints or publishes any matter in contravention of the provisions contained insub-section (1), he shall be punishable with fine which may extend to one thousand rupees.

34. Duty of Court in passing decrees.-(1) In any proceeding under Chapter V or Chapter VI, whether defended or not, if the Court if satisfied that,-

(a)any of the grounds for granting relief exists; and

(b)where the petition is founded on the ground specified in Cl.(a) of sub-section (1) of Sec. 27, the petitioner has not in any manner been accessory to or connived at or condoned the act of sexual intercourse referred to therein or where the ground of the petition is cruelty, the petitioner has not in any manner condoned the cruelty; and

(c)when divorce is sought on the ground of mutual consent, such consent has not been obtained by force, fraud or undue influence; and

(d)the petition is not presented or prosecuted in collusion with the respondent; and

(e)there has not been any unnecessary or improper delay in instituting the proceedings; and

(f)there is no other legal ground why the relief should not be granted; then, and in such a case, but not otherwise, the Court shall decree such relief accordingly.

(2) Before proceeding to grant any relief under this Act it shall be the duty of the Court in the first instance, in every case where it is possible so to do consistently with the nature and circumstances of the case, to make every endeavour to bring about a reconciliation between the parties :

Provided that nothing contained in this sub-section shall apply to any proceeding wherein relief is sought on any of the grounds specified in Cls. (c), (e), (f), (g) and (h) of sub-section (1) of Sec.27.

(3) For the purpose of aiding the Court in bringing about such reconciliation, the Court may, if the parties so desire or if the Court thinks it just and proper so to do, adjourn the proceedings for a reasonable period not exceeding fifteen days, and refer the matter to any person named by the parties in this behalf or to any person nominated by the Court if the parties fail to name any person, with directions to report to the Court as to whether reconciliation can be and has been effected and the Court shall in disposing of the proceeding have due regard to the report.

(4) In every case where a marriage is dissolved by a decree of divorce, the Court passing the decree shall give a copy thereof free of cost to each of the parties.

35.Relief for respondent in divorce and other proceedings.-- In any proceeding for divorce or judicial separation or restitution of conjugal rights, the respondent may not only oppose the relief sought on the ground of petitioner's adultery, cruelty or desertion, but also make counter- claim for any relief under this Act on that ground, and if the petitioner's adultery, cruelty or desertion is proved, the Court may give to the respondent any relief under this Act to which he or she would have been entitled if he or she had presented a petition seeking such relief on that ground.

36.Alimony pendente lite.-- Where in any proceeding under Chapter V or Chapter VI it appears to the District Court that the wife has no independent income sufficient for her support and the necessary expenses of the proceeding, it may, on the application of the wife, order the husband to pay to her the expenses of the proceeding, and weekly or monthly during the proceeding such sum as having regard to the husband's income, it may seem to the Court to be reasonable.

37.Permanent alimony and maintenance.--(1) Any Court exercising jurisdiction under Chapter V or Chapter VI may, at the time of passing any decree or at any time subsequent to the decree, on application made to it for the purpose, order that the husband shall secure to the wife for her maintenance and support, if necessary, by a charge on the husband's property, such gross sum or such monthly or periodical payment of money for a term not exceeding her life, as having regard to her own property, if any, her husband's property and ability, the conduct of the parties and other circumstances of the case it may seem to the Court to be just.

(2)If the District Court is satisfied that there is a change in the circumstances of either party at any time after it has made an order under sub-section (1), it may at the instance of either party, vary, modify or rescind any such order in such manner as it may seem to the Court to be just.

(3)If the District Court is satisfied that the wife in whose favour an order has been made under this section has remarried or is not leading a chaste life, it may, at the instance of the husband vary, modify or rescind any such order and in such manner as the Court may deem just.

38.Custody of children.-- In any proceeding under Chapter V or Chapter VI the District Court may, from time to time, pass such interim orders and make such provisions in the decree as it may seem to it to be just and proper with respect to the custody, maintenance and education of minor children, consistently with their wishes wherever possible, and may, after the decree, upon application by petition for the purpose, make, revoke, suspend or vary, from time to time, all such orders and provisions with respect to the custody, maintenance and education of such children as might have been made by such decree or interim orders in case the proceeding for obtaining such decree were still pending.

39.Appeals from decrees and orders.--(1) All decrees made by the Court in any proceeding under Chapter V or Chapter VI shall, subject to the provisions of sub-section (3), be appealable as decrees of the Court made in the exercise of its original civil jurisdiction, and such appeal shall lie to the Court to which appeals ordinarily lie from the decisions of the Court given in the exercise of its original civil jurisdiction.

(2)Orders made by the Court in any proceeding under this Act under Sec.37 or Sec.38 shall subject to the provisions of Sub-section (3), be appealable if they are not interim orders, and every such appeal shall lie to the Court to which appeals ordinarily lie from the decisions of the Court given in the exercise of its original civil jurisdiction.

(3)There shall be no appeal under this section on the subject of the costs only.

(4)Every appeal under this section shall be preferred within a period of thirty days from the date of the decree or order.

39-A. Enforcement of decrees and orders.-- All decrees and orders made by the Court in any proceeding under Chapter V or Chapter VI shall be enforced in the like manner as the decrees and orders of the Court made in the exercise of its original civil jurisdiction for the time being are enforced.

40. Application of Act 5 of 1908.-- Subject to the other provisions contained in this Act, and to such rules as the High Court may make in this behalf, all proceedings under this Act shall be regulated, as far as may be, by the Code of Civil Procedure, 1908.

40-A. Power to transfer petitions in certain cases.--(1) Where--

(a)a petition under this Act has been presented to the District Court having jurisdiction by a party to the marriage praying for a decree for judicial separation under Sec.23 or for a decree of divorce under Sec.27, and

(b)another petition under this act has been presented thereafter by the other party to the marriage praying for decree for judicial separation under Sec.23, or for decree of divorce under Sec.27 on any ground whether in the same District Court or in a different District Court, in the same State or in a different State.

the petition shall be dealt with as specified in sub-section (2).

(2) In a case where sub-section (1) applies.--

(a)if the petitions are presented to the same District Court, both the petitions shall be tried and heard together by that District Court :

(b)if the petitions are presented to different District Courts the petition presented later shall be transferred to the District Court in which the earlier petition was presented and both the petitions shall be heard and disposed of together by the District Court in which the earlier petition was presented.

(3) In a case where Cl. (b) of sub-section (2) applies, the Court or the Government, as the case may be, competent under the Code of Civil Procedure, 1908 (5 of 1908), to transfer any suit or proceeding from the District Court in which the later petition has been presented to the District Court in which the earlier petition is pending shall exercise its powers to transfer such later petition as if it had been empowered so to do under the said Code.

40-B. Special provision relating to trial and disposal of petitions under the Act.-(1) The trial of a petition under this Act shall so far as is practicable consistently with the interests of justice in respect of the trial, be continued from day to day until its conclusion, unless the Court finds the adjournment of the trial beyond the following day to be necessary for reasons to be recorded.

(2)Every petition under this Act shall be tried as expeditiously as possible and endeavour shall be made to conclude the trial within six months from the date of service of notice of the petition on the respondent.

(3)Every appeal under this Act shall be heard as expeditiously as possible, and endeavour shall be made to conclude the hearing within three months from the date of service of notice of appeal on the respondent.

40-C. Documentary evidence.-- Notwithstanding anything contained in any enactment to the contrary, no document shall be inadmissible in evidence in any proceeding at the trial of a petition under this Act on the ground that it is not duly stamped or registered.

41. Power of High Court to make rules regulating procedure.--(1) The High Court shall, by notification in the Official Gazette, make such rules consistent with the provisions contained in this Act and the Code of Civil Procedure, 1908 (5 of 1908), as it may consider expedient for the

purpose of carrying into effect the provisions of Chapters V, VI and VII.

(2) In particular, and without prejudice to the generality of the foregoing provision, such rules shall provide for.--

(a)the impleading by the petitioner of the adulterer as a co-respondent on a petition for divorce on the ground of adultery, and the circumstances in which the petitioner may be excused from doing so:

(b)the awarding of damages against any such co-respondent,

(c) the intervention in any proceeding under Chapter V or Chapter VI by any person not already a party thereto :

(d)the form and contents of petitions for nullity of marriage or for divorce and the payment of costs incurred by parties to such petitions ; and

(e)any other matter for which no provision or no sufficient provision is made in this Act, and for which provision is made in the Indian Divorce Act, 1869 (4 of 1869).

42.Saving.-- Nothing contained in this Act shall affect the validity of any marriage not solemnized under its provisions; not shall this Act be deemed directly or indirectly to affect the validity of any mode of contracting marriage.

43.Penalty on married person marrying again under this Act.-- Save as otherwise provided in Chapter III, every person who, being at the time married procures a marriage of himself or herself to be solemnized under this Act shall be deemed to have committed an offence under Sec. 494 or Sec. 495 of the Indian Penal Code 1860 (45 of 1860), as the case may be, and the marriage so solemnized shall be void.

44.Punishment of bigamy.-- Every person whose marriage is solemnized under this Act and who, during the lifetime of his or her wife or husband, contracts any other marriage shall be subject to the penalties provided in Secs.494 and 495 of the Indian Penal Code, 1860 (45 of 1860) for the offence of marrying again during the lifetime of a husband of wife, and the marriage so contracted shall be void.

45.Penalty for signing false declaration or certificate.-- Every person making, signing or attesting any declaration or certificate required by or under this Act containing a statement which is false and which he either knows or believes to be false or does not believe to be true shall be guilty of the offence described in Sec.199 of the Indian Penal Code, 1860 (45 of 1860).

46.Penalty for wrongful action of Marriage Officer.-- Any Marriage Officer who knowingly and willfully solemnizes a marriage under this Act,--

(1)without publishing a notice regarding such marriage as required by Sec.5 ; or

(2)within thirty days of the publication of the notice such marriage; or

(3)in contravention of any other provision contained in this Act, shall be punishable with simple imprisonment for a term which may extend to one year, or with fine which may extend to five hundred rupees, or with both.

47. Marriage Certificate Book to be open to inspection--(1) The Marriage Certificate Book kept under this Act shall at all reasonable times be open for inspection and shall be admissible as evidence of the statements therein contained.

(2) Certified extracts from the Marriage Certificate Book shall, on application, be given by the Marriage Officer to the applicant on payment by him of the prescribed fee.

48. Transmission of copies of entries in marriage records.-- Every Marriage Officer in a State shall send to Registrar-General of Births, Deaths and Marriages of that State at such intervals and in such form as may be prescribed, a true copy of all entries made by him in the

Marriage Certificate Book since the last of such intervals, and in the case of Marriage Officers outside the territories to which this Act extends, the true copy shall be sent to such authority as the Central Government may specify in this behalf.

49. Correction of errors.--(1) Any Marriage Officer who discovers any error in the form or substance of any entry in the Marriage Certificate Book may, within one month next after the discovery of such error, in the presence of the persons married, or in case of their death or absence, in the presence of two other credible witnesses, correct the error by entry in the margin without any alteration of the original entry and shall sign the marginal entry and add thereto the date of such correction and the Marriage Officer shall make the like marginal entry in the certificate thereof.

(2) Every correction made under this section shall be attested by the witnesses in whose presence it was made.

(3) Where a copy of any entry has already been sent under Sec. 48 to the Registrar-General or other authority the Marriage Officer shall make and send in the like manner a separate certificate of the original erroneous entry and of the marginal corrections therein made.

50. Power to make rules.--(1) The Central Government, in the case of officers of the Central Government, and the State Government, in all other cases, may, by notification in the Official Gazette, make rules for carrying out the purposes of this Act.

(2) In particular, and without prejudice to the generality of the foregoing power, such rules may provide for all or any of the following matters, namely:

(a)the duties and powers of Marriage Officers and the areas in which they may exercise jurisdiction;

(b)the manner in which a Marriage Officer may hold inquiries under this Act and the procedure therefore:

(c)the form and manner in which any books required by or under this Act shall be maintained:

(d)the fees that may be levied for the performance of any duty imposed upon a Marriage Officer under this Act;

(e)the manner in which public notice shall be given under Sec. 16:

(f)the form in which, and the intervals within which, copies of entries in the Marriage Certificate Book shall be sent in pursuance of Sec.48:

(g)any other matter which may be or requires to be prescribed.

(3)Every rule made by the Central Government under this Act shall be laid, as soon as may be after it is made, before each House of Parliament, while it is in session, for a total period of thirty days which may be comprised in one session or in two or more successive sessions, and if, before the expiry of the session immediately following the session or the successive sessions aforesaid, both Houses agree in making any modification in the rule or both Houses agree that the rule should not be made, the rule shall thereafter have effect only in such modified form, or be of no effect as the case may be; so, however, that any such modification or annulment shall be without prejudice to the validity of anything previously done under that rule.

(4)Every rule made by the State Government under this Act shall be laid, as soon as it is made, before the State Legislature.

51. Repeals and savings.-(1) The Special Marriage Act, 1872 (3 of 1872), and any law corresponding to the Special Marriage Act, 1872, in force in any Part B State immediately before the commencement of this Act are hereby repealed.

(2) Notwithstanding such repeal.-

(a) all marriages duly solemnized under Special Marriage Act, 1872 (3 of 1872) or any such corresponding law shall be deemed to have been solemnized under this Act:

(b) all suits and proceeding in causes and matters matrimonial which, when this Act comes into operation, are pending in any Court shall be dealt with and decided by such Court, so far as may be, as if they had been originally instituted therein under this Act.

(3) The provisions of sub-section (2) shall be without prejudice to the provisions contained in Sec. 6 of the General Clauses Act, 1897 (10 of 1897) which shall also apply to the repeal of the corresponding law as if such corresponding law had been an enactment.

THE HINDU ADOPTIONS AND MAINTENANCE ACT, 1956

[Act No.78 of 1956][21st December, 1956]

Be it enacted by Parliament in the Seventh Year of the Republic of India as follows:-

CHAPTER I

PRELIMINARY

1. Short title and extent- (1) This Act may be called the Hindu Adoptions and Maintenance Act, 1956.

(2) It extends to the whole of India except the State of Jammu and Kashmir.

2. Application of Act- (1) This Act applies-

(a)to any person, who is a Hindu by religion in any of its forms or developments, including a Virashaiva, a Lingayat or a follower of the Brahmo, Prarthana or Arya Samaj,

(b)to any person who is a Buddhist, Jaina or Sikh by religion, and

(c)to any other person who is not a Muslim, Christian, Parsi or Jew by religion unless it is proved that any such person would not have been governed by the Hindu law or by any custom or usage as part of that law in respect of any of the matters dealt with herein if this Act had not been passed.

Explanation- The following persons are Hindus, Buddhists, Jainas or Sikhs by religion, as the case may be:-

(a)any child, legitimate or illegitimate, both of whose parents are Hindus, Buddhists, Jainas or Sikhs by religion;

(b)any child, legitimate for illegitin~ate, one of whose parents is a Hindu, Buddhist, Jaina or Sikh by religion and who is brought up as a member of the tribe, community, group or family to which such parent belongs or belonged,

(bb) any child, legitimate or illegitimate, who has been abandoned both by his father and mother or whose parentage is not known and who is either case is brought up as a Hindu, Buddhist, Jaina or Sikh, and

(c) any person who is a convert or reconvert to the Hindu, Buddhist, Jaina or Sikh, religion.

(2) Notwithstanding anything contained in sub-section (1), nothing contained in this Act shall apply to the members of any Scheduled Tribe within the meaning of clause (25) of Article 366 of the Constitution unless the Central Government,

by notification in the Official Gazette, otherwise directs.

(2-A) Notwithstanding anything contained in sub-section (1), nothing contained in this Act shall apply to the Renoncants of the Union Territory of Pondicherry.

(3) The expression "Hindu" in any portion of this Act shall be construed as if it included a person who, though not a Hindu by religion, is nevertheless, a person to whom this Act applies by virtue of the provisions contained in this section.

3. Definitions- In this Act unless the context otherwise requires-

(a) the expressions "custom" and "usage" signify any rule which, having been continuously and uniformly observed for a long time, has obtained the force of law among Hindus in any local area, tribe, community, group or family;

Provided that the rule is certain and not unreasonable or opposed to public policy; and

Provided further that, in the case of a rule applicable only to a family, it has not been discontinued by the family;

(b) "maintenance" includes-

(i) in all cases, provision for food, clothing, residence, education and medical attendance and treatment;

(ii) in the case of an unmarried daughter also the reasonable expenses of and incident to her marriage;

(c) "minor" means a person who has not completed his or her age of eighteen years.

4. Overriding effect of Act- Save as otherwise expressly provided in this Act,-

(a)any text, rule or interpretation of Hindu law or any custom or usage as part of that law in force immediately before the commencement of this Act shall cease to have effect with respect to any matter for which provision is made in this Act;

(b)any other law in force immediately before the commencement of this Act shall cease to apply to Hindus in so far as it is inconsistent with any of the provisions contained in this Act.

CHAPTER II

ADOPTION

5. Adoptions to be regulated by this Chapter- (1) No adoption shall be made after the commencement of this Act by or to a Hindu except in accordance with the provisions contained in this Chapter, and any adoption made in contravention of the said provisions shall be void.

(2) An adoption which is void shall neither create any rights in the adoptive family in favour of any person which he or she could not have acquired except by reason of the adoption, nor destroy the rights of any person in the family of his or her birth.

6. Requisites of a valid adoption- No adoption shall be valid unless-

(i)the person adopting has the capacity, and also the right, to take in adoption;

(ii)the person giving in adoption has the capacity to do so;

(iii)the person adopted is capable of being taken in adoption; and

(iv)the adoption is made in compliance with the other conditions mentioned in this Chapter.

7. Capacity of a male Hindu to take in adoption- Any male Hindu who is of sound mind and is not a minor has the capacity to take a son or a daughter in adoption.

Provided that, if he has a wife living, he shall not adopt except with the consent of his wife unless the wife has completely and finally renounced the world or has ceased to be a Hindu or has been declared by a court of competent jurisdiction to be of unsound mind.

Explanation-If a person has more than one wife living at the time of adoption, the consent of all the wives is necessary unless the consent of any one of them is unnecessary for any of the reasons specified in the preceding proviso.

8. Capacity of a female Hindu to take in adoption- Any female Hindu-

(a)who is of sound mind,

(b)who is not a minor, and

(c)who is not married, or if married, whose marriage has been dissolved or whose husband is dead or has completely and finally renounced the world or has ceased to be a Hindu or has been declared by a court of competent jurisdiction to be of unsound mind,

has the capacity to take a son or daughter in adoption.

9. Persons capable of giving in adoption- (1) No person except the father or mother or the guardian of a child shall have the capacity to give the child in adoption.

(2)Subject to the provisions of sub-section (3) and sub-section (4), the father, if alive, shall alone have the right to give in adoption, but such right shall not be exercised save with the consent of the mother unless the mother has completely and finally renounced the world or has ceased to be a Hindu or has been declared by a court of competent jurisdiction to be of unsound mind.

(3)The mother may give the child in adoption if the father is dead or has completely and finally renounced the world or has ceased to be a Hindu or has

been declared by a court of competent jurisdiction to be of unsound mind.

(4)Where both the father and mother are dead or have completely and finally renounced the world or have abandoned the child or have been declared by a court of competent jurisdiction to be of unsound mind or where the parentage of the child is not known, the guardian of the child may give the child in adoption with the previous permission of the court to any person including the guardian himself.

(5)Before granting permission to a guardian under sub-section (4) the court shall be satisfied that the adoption will be for the welfare of the child, due consideration being for this purpose given to the wishes of the child having regard to the age and understanding of the child and that the applicant for permission has not received or agreed to receive and that no person has made or given or agreed to make or give to the applicant any payment or reward in consideration of the adoption except such as the court may sanction.

Explanation- For the purposes of this section-

(i) the expressions "father" and "mother" do not include an adoptive father and an adoptive mother,

(i-a) "guardian" means aperson having the care of the person of a child or of both his person and property and includes-

(a)a guardian appointed by will of the child's father or mother; and

(b)a guardian appointed or declared by a court; and

(ii) "court" means the city or civil court or a district court within the local limits or whose jurisdiction the child to be adopted ordinarily resides.

10. Persons who may be adopted- No person shall be capable of being taken in adoption unless the following conditions are fulfilled, namely-

(i)he or she is a Hindu;

(ii)he or she has not already been adopted;

(iii)he or she has not been married, unless there is a custom or usage applicable to the parties which permits persons who are married being taken in adoption;

(iv)he or she has not completed the age of fifteen years, unless there is a custom or usage applicable to the parties which permits persons who have completed the age of fifteen years being taken in adoption.

11. Other conditions for a valid adoption- In every adoption, the following conditions must be complied with:

(i) if any adoption is of a son, the adoptive father or mother by whom the adoption is made must not have a Hindu son, son's son or son's son's son (whether by legitimate blood relationship or by adoption) living at the time of

adoption;

(ii)if the adoption is of a daughter the adoptive father or mother by whom the adoption is made must not have a Hindu daughter or son's daughter (whether by legitimate blood relationship or by adoption) living at the time of adoption;

(iii)if the adoption is by a male and the person to be adopted is a female, the adoptive father is at least twenty-one years older than the person to be adopted;

(iv)if the adoption is by a female and the person to be adopted is a male, the adoptive mother is at least twenty-one years older than the person to be adopted;

(v)the same child may not be adopted simultaneously by two or more persons;

(vi)the child to be adopted must be actually given and taken in adoption by the parents or guardian concerned or under their authority with intent to transfer the child from the family of its birth or in the case of an abandoned child or a child whose parentage is not known, from the place or family where it has been brought up to the family of its adoption.

Provided that the performance of *datta homan,* shall not be essential to the validity of an adoption.

12. Effect of adoptions- An adopted child shall be deemed to be the child of his or her adoptive father or mother for all purposes with effect from the date of the adoption and from such date all the ties of the child in the family of his or her birth shall be deemed to be severed and replaced by those created by the adoption in the adoptive family.

Provided that-

(a)the child cannot marry any person whom he or she could not have married if he or she had continued in the family of his or her birth;

(b)any property which vested in the adopted child before the adoption shall continue to vest in such person subject to the obligations, if any, attaching to the ownership of such property, including the obligation to maintain relatives in the family of his or her birth;

(c)the adopted child shall not divest any person of any estate which vested in him or her before the adoption.

13.Right of adoptive parents to dispose of their properties- Subject to any agreement to the contrary, an adoption does not deprive the adoptive father or mother of the power to dispose of his or her property by transfer *inter vivos*or by will.

14.Determination of adoptive mother in certain cases- (1) Where a Hindu who has a wife living adopts a child she shall be deemed to be the adoptive mother.

(2) Where an adoption has been made with the consent of more than one wife,

the senior most in marriage among them shall be deemed to be the adoptive mother and the others to be stepmothers.

(3)Where a widower or a bachelor adopts a child, any wife whom he subsequently marries shall be deemed to be the stepmother of the adopted child.

(4)Where a widow or an unmarried woman adopts a child, any husband whom she marries subsequently shall be deemed to be the stepfather of the adopted child.

15.Valid adoption not to be cancelled- No adoption which had been validly made can be cancelled by the adoptive father or mother or any other person, nor can the adopted child renounce his or her status as such and return to the family of his or her birth.

16.Presumption as to registered documents relating to adoption- Whenever any document registered under any law for the time being in force is produced before any court purporting to record an adoption made and is signed by the person giving and the person taking the child in adoption, the court shall presume that the adoption has been made in compliance with the provisions of this Act unless and until it is disproved.

17.Prohibition of certain payments- (1) No person shall receive or agree to receive any payment or other reward in consideration of the adoption of any person, and no person shall make or give or agree to make or give to any other person any payment or reward the receipt of which is prohibited by this section.

(2)If any person contravenes the provisions of sub-section (1), he shall be punishable with imprisonment which may extend to six months, or with fine, or with both.

(3)No prosecution under this section shall be instituted without the previous sanction of the State Government or an officer authorized by the State Government in this behalf.

CHAPTER III

MAINTENANCE

18. Maintenance of wife- (1) Subject to the provisions of this section, a Hindu wife, whether married before or after the commencement of this Act, shall be entitled to be maintained by her husband during her lifetime.

(2) A Hindu wife shall be entitled to live separately from her husband without forfeiting her claim to maintenance,-

(a)if he is guilty of desertion, that is to say, of abandoning her without reasonable cause and without her consent or against her wish, or of wilfully neglecting her;

(b)if he has treated her with such cruelty as to cause a reasonable apprehension in her mind that it will be harmful or injurious to live with her husband;

(c)if he is suffering from a virulent form of leprosy;

(d)if he has any other wife living;

(e)if he keeps a concubine in the same house in which his wife is living or habitually resides with a concubine elsewhere;

(f)if he has ceased to be a Hindu by conversion to another religion;

(g)if there is any other cause justifying her living separately.

(3) A Hindu wife shall not be entitled to separate residence and maintenance from her husband if she is unchaste or ceases to be a Hindu by conversion to another religion.

19. Maintenance of widowed daughter-in-law- (1) A Hindu wife, whether married before or after the commencement of this Act, shall be entitled to be maintained after the death of her husband by her father-in-law.

Provided and to the extent that she is unable to maintain herself out of her own earnings or other property or, where she has no property of her own, is unable to obtain maintenance-

(a)from the estate of her husband or her father or mother, or

(b)from her son or daughter, if any, or his or her estate.

(2) Any obligation under sub-section (1) shall not be enforceable if the fatherin- law has not the means to do so from any coparcenary property in his possession out of which the daughter-in-law has not obtained any share, and any such obligation shall cease on the remarriage of the daughter-in-law.

20. Maintenance of children and aged parents- (1) Subject to the provisions of this section a Hindu is bound, during his or her lifetime, to maintain his or her legitimate or illegitimate children and his or her aged or infirm parents.

(2)A legitimate or illegitimate child may claim maintenance from his or her father or mother so long as the child is a minor.

(3)The obligation of a person to maintain his or her aged or infirm parent or daughter who is unmarried extends in so far as the parent or the unmarried daughter, as the case may be, is unable to maintain himself or herself out of his or her own ealnings or other property

Explanation- In this section "parent" includes a childless stepmother.

21. Dependents defined- For the purposes of this Chapter "dependents" mean the following relatives of the deceased-

(i)his or her father;

(ii)his or her mother;

(iii)his widow, so long as she does not remarry;

(iv)his or her son or the son of his predeceased son or the son of a predeceased son of his predeceased son, so long as he is a minor; provided and to the extent that he is unable to obtain maintenance, in the case of a grandson from his father's or mother's estate, and in the case of a great-grandson, from the estate of his father or mother or father's father or father's mother;

(v)his or her unmarried daughter for the unmarried daughter of his predeceased son or the unmarried daughter of a predeceased son of his predeceased son, so long as she remains unmarried; provided and to the extent that she is unable to obtain maintenance, in the case of a grand daughter from her father's or mother's estate and in the case of a great-grand daughter from the estate of her father or mother or father's father or father's mother;

(vi)his widowed daughter; provided and to the extent that she is unable to obtain maintenance-

(a)from the estate of her husband; or

(b)from her son or daughter, if any, or his or her estate; or

(c)from her father-in-law or his father or the estate of either of them;

(vii)any widow of his son or of a son of his predeceased son, so long as she does not remarry; provided and to the extent that she is unable to obtain maintenance from her husband's estate, or from her son or daughter, if any, or his or her estate; or in the case of a grandson's widow, also from her father-in-law's estate;

(viii)his or her minor illegitimate son, so long as he remains a minor;

(xi) his or her illegitimate daughter, so long as she remains unmarried.

22. Maintenance of dependents- (1) Subject to the provisions of sub-section(2), the heirs of a deceased Hindu are bound to maintain the dependents of the deceased out of the estate inherited by them from the deceased.

(2)Where a dependent has not obtained, by testamentary or intestate succession, any share in the estate of a Hindu dying after the commencement of this Act, the dependent shall be entitled, subject to the provisions of this Act, to maintenance from those who take the estate.

(3)The liability of each of the persons who take the estate shall be in proportion to the value of the share or part of the estate taken by him or her.

(4)Notwithstanding anything contained in sub-section (2) or sub-section (3), no person who is himself or herself a dependent shall be liable to contribute to the maintenance of others, if he or she has obtained a share or part, the value of which is, or would, if the liability to contribute were enforced, become less than

what would be awarded to him or her by way of maintenance under this Act.

23. Amount of maintenance- (1) It shall be in the discretion of the court to determine whether any, and if so what, maintenance shall be awarded under the provisions of this Act, and in doing so, the court shall have due regard to the consideration set out in sub-section (2) or sub-section (3), as the case maybe, so far as they are applicable.

(2) In determining the amount of maintenance, if any, to be awarded to a wife, children or aged or infirm parents under this Act, regard shall be had to-

(a)the position and status of the parties;

(b)the reasonable wants of the claimant;

(c)if the claimant is living separately, whether the claimant is justified in doing

so;

(d)the value of the claimant's property and any income derived from such property, or from the claimant's own earning or from any other source;

(e)the number of persons entitled to maintenance under this Act.

(3) In determining the amount of maintenance, if any, to be awarded to a dependent under this Act, regard shall be had to-

(a)the net value of the estate of the deceased after providing for the payment of his debts;

(b)the provision, if any, made under a will of the deceased in respect, of the dependent;

(c)the degree of relationship between the two;

(d)the reasonable wants of the dependent;

(e)the past relations between the dependent and the deceased;

(f)the value of the property of the dependent and any income derived from such property, or from his or her earnings or from any other course;

(g)the number of dependents entitled to maintenance under this Act.

24.Claimant to maintenance should be a Hindu- No person shall be entitled to claim maintenance under this Chapter if he or she has ceased to be a Hindu by conversion to another religion.

25.Amount of maintenance may be altered on change of circumstances- Theamount of maintenance, whether fixed by a decree of court or by agreement either before or after the commencement of this Act, may be altered subsequently if there is a material change in the circumstances justifying such alteration.

26.Debts to have priority-Subject to the provisions contained in Section 27 debts of every description contracted or payable by the deceased shall have priority over the claims of his dependents for maintenance under this Act.

27.Maintenance when to be a charge- A dependent's claim for maintenance under this Act shall not be a charge on the estate of the deceased or any portion thereof, unless one has been created by the will of the deceased, by a decree of court, by agreement between the dependent and the owner of the estate or portion, or otherwise.

28.Effect of transfer of property on right or maintenance- where a dependent has a right to receive maintenance out of an estate and such estate or any part thereof is transferred, the right to receive maintenance may be enforced agamst the transferee if the transferee has notice of the right or if the transfer is gratuitous; but not against the transferee for consideration and without notice of the right.

CHAPTER IV

REPEALS AND SAVINGS

29.Repeals- [Repealed by Act 58 of 1960].

30.Savings- Nothing contained in this Act shall affect any adoption made before the commencement of this Act, and the validity and effect of any such adoption shall be determined as if this Act had not been passed

THE DOWRY PROHIBITION ACT, 1961

An Act to prohibit the giving or taking of dowry

Be it enacted by Parliament in the Twelfth Year of the Republic of India as follows :

1. Short title, extent and commencement.---

(1)This Act may be called the Dowry Prohibition Act, 1961.

(2)It extends to the whole of India except the State of Jammu and Kashmir.

(3)It shall come into force on such date as the Central Government may, by notification in the official Gazette, appoint.

2. Definition of "dowry".-in this Act, "dowry" means any property or valuable security given or agreed to be given either directly or indirectly---

(a)by one party to a marriage to the other party to the marriage; or (b)by the persons of either party to a marriage or by any other person, to either party to the marriage or to any other person;

at or before [or any time after the marriages] [in connection with the marriage of said parties but does not include] dower or mahr in the case of persons to whom the Muslim Personal Law (Shariat) applies.

Explanation II.-The expression "valuable security" has the same meaning as in Sec. 30 of the Indian Penal Code (45 of 1860).

State Amendment

Haryana.-Substitution of Sec. 2 of Parliament Act 28 of 1961.-For Sec. 2 of the Dowry Prohibition Act, 1961, the following section shall be substituted, namely :

"2. Definitions.-In this Act, unless the context otherwise requires-

(i) "dowry" means any property or valuable security given or agreed to be given either directly or indirectly-

(a) by one party to a marriage to the other party to the marriage; or

(b) by the parents of either party to a marriage or by any other person, to either party to the marriage or to any other person ;

at or before or after the marriage as consideration for the marriage of the said parties, but does not include dower or mahr in case of person to whom the Muslim Personal Law (Shariat) applies.

Explanation I.-For the removal of doubts it is hereby declared that any presents made at the time of a marriage to either party to the marriage in the form of cash, ornaments, clothes, or other articles, shall not be deemed to be dowry within the meaning of the section, unless they are made as consideration for the marriage of the said parties.

Explanation II.-The expression "valuable securities" has the same meaning as in Sec. 30 of the Indian Penal Code (45 of 1860).

(ii) "marriage expenses" shall include expenses incurred directly or indirectly at or before the marriage on

(a)thakka, sagai, tikka, shagun and milni ceremonies;

(b)the gifts made by one party to a marriage to the other _party to the marriage or by the parents, grand-parents and brothers of either party to a marriage, to either party to the marriage or the blood relations thereof.

(c)illumination, food and the arrangements for serving food to the members of the marriage party and other expenses incidental thereto.

Explanation .-For the removal of doubts, it is hereby declared that any gifts, made by a person other than those specified in sub-clause (b), at the time of the marriage to either party to the marriage shall not be deemed to be marriage expenses.

Comments

Dowry-What amounts to.-It was contended, in the instant case, that the definition of the term "dowry' as given in Sec. 2 should include even a demand made by one party though the other party would not agree to pay that amount. It is impossible to think that such construction is possible. Section 2 has specifically defined the term "dowry' and that definition has to be borne in mind whenever the rest of the provisions of the Act are to be interpreted, particularly where those provisions contain the word "dowry". It is for this purpose that the Legislature has taken care to define the term "dowry". Thus it would not be ordinarily open to anybody to contend that the term "dowry" should be interpreted in a manner other than mentioned in Sec. 2.'

The furnishing of a list of ornaments and other household articles, such as, refrigerator, furniture, electric appliances, etc., at the time of the settlement of the marriage amounts to demand of dowry within the meaning of Sec. 2 of the Dowry Prohibition Act, 1961. That being so, the High Court ought to have considered the appeal on rnerits and decided as to whether the respondents were guilty of offences punishable under Sec. 406 of the Indian Penal Code, 1860, read with Secs. 4 and 6 and Dowry Prohibition Act, 1961, by the wrongful retention to the articles given as marriage gifts, while driving out the appellant from the matrimonial house. The High Court would also ensure that all the articles to the wife at the time of the marriage, including the valuable gold ornaments, are restored to her. Meaning of dowry defined.-Articles received as presents and gifts at the time of marriage cannot be termed as dowry.

3

Amount paid to the prospective son-in-law for purchase of property on the joint names of daughter and the would-be son-in-law whether amounts to dowry.- In

Kunju Moideen v. Sayed Mohammed, on a fair reading of the plaint, it is evident that the amount that was paid, was for purchase of property in the name of the plaintiff's daughter and the would-be son-in-law. It cannot be said that the amount was paid or agreed to be paid at or before or after the marriage as consideration for the marriage of the parties. On that short ground the amounts sought to be recovered by the plaintiff is not dowry and it will not come within the inhibition of Dowry Prohibition Act. The learned Subordinate Judge was in error in holding that it will come within the definition of the Act and in non-suiting the plaintiff.

Dowry Prohibition Act, whether bars the traditional giving of presents- The Dowry Prohibition Act does not, in any way, bar the traditional giving of present at or about the time of the wedding which may be willing and affection are gifts by parents and close relations of the bride to her. Such presents or dowry given by the parents is, therefore, not at all within the definition of the aforesaid statute. Indeed this traditional giving of presents at or about the time of wedding is an accepted practice which finds mention in the oldest of Hindu scriptures and is continued today with a greater zeal. Consequently, dowry as commonly understood is something different and alien to the peculiar definition thereof in the Dowry Prohibition Act. A voluntary and affectionate giving of dowry and traditional presents would thus be plainly out of the ambit of the particular definition under the Act and once that is so the rest of the provisions thereof would be equally inapplicable. Consequently the argument that the applicability of the special provisions of the Dowry Prohibition Act would exclude the general provisions of the Indian Penal Code would not even arise and in any case has no validity.

Offences under the Dowry Prohibitin Act and under Sec. 406, I.P.C., whether can stand together on the same set on facts.- A plain reading of the definition of dowry would show that it means any property given directly as a consideration for the marriage of the parties. Now once that is so, dowry of this kind is in fact a quid pro quo for the marriage itself. Inevitably it would follow that whatsoever is given consideration for the marriage itself cannot possibly be deemed in the eye of law as an entrustment or passing of dominion over property. To recall the familiar analogy of the law of contract, the consideration is the price for the promise and therefore, such property cannot be deemed even remotely to have been entrusted or dominion passed over it to the other. The necessary result, therefore, is that the same set of facts allegedly constituting an offence under the Dowry Prohibition Act cannot possibly come within the ambit of Sec. 106, I.P.C. This would be plainly a consideration in terms. One offence is tested on property forming the consideration for the marriage as such, whilst, the other visualises the entrustment and passing of dominion over property individually owned. The

4

offences under the Dowry Prohibition Act cannot under Sec. 406, I.P.C., thus cannot stand together on the same set of facts.

Interpretation of section.-The Court can merely interpret the section - it cannot re- write,re-cast or re-design the section.

3. Penalty for giving or taking dowry.- [(1)] If any person, after the commencement of this Act, gives or takes or abets the giving or taking of dowry, he shall be punishable [with imprisonment for a term which shall

not be less than [five years], and with fine which shall not be less than fifteen thousand rupees or the amount of the value of such dowry, whichever is more :

Provided that the Court may, for adequate and special reasons to be recorded in the judgment, impose a sentence of imprisonment for a term of less than [five years].

[(2)] Nothing in sub-section (1) shall apply to or, in relation to,-

(a)presents which are given at the time of a marriage to the bride (without any demand having been made in that behalf): Provided that such presents are entered in list maintained in accordance with rule made under this Act ;

(b)presents which are given at the time of marriage to the bridegroom (without any demand having been made in that behalf) :

Provided that such presents are entered in a list maintained in accordance with the rules made under this Act :

Provided further that where such presents are made by or on behalf of the bride or any person related to the bride, such presents are of a customary nature and the value thereof is not excessive having regard to the financial status of the person by whom, or on whose behalf, such presents are given.]

The Medical Termination Of Pregnancy Act, 1971

(Act No. 34 of 1971)

An Act to provide for the termination of certain pregnancies by registered medical practitioners and for matters connected therewith or incidental thereto

Be it enacted by Parliament in the Twenty-second Year of the Republic of India as follows:

1. Short title, extent and commencement.-

(1)This Act may be called the Medical Termination of Pregnancy Act, 1971.

(2)It extends to the whole of India except the State of Jammu and Kashmir.

(3)It shall come into force on such date as the Central Government may, by notification in the Official Gazette,

appoint.

2.Definitions.-In this Act, unless the context otherwise requires,-

(a)"guardian" means a person having the care of the person of a minor or a lunatic;

(b)"lunatic" has the meaning assigned to it in Sec.3 of the Indian Lunacy Act, 1912 (4 of 1912) ;

(c)"minor" means a person who, under the provisions of the Indian Majority Act, 1875 (9 of 1875), is to be deemed not to have attained his majority,

(d) "registered medical practitioner" means a medical practitioner who possesses any recognized medical qualification as defined in Cl.(h) of Sec. 2 of the Indian Medical Council Act, 1956 (102 of 1956), whose name has been entered in a State Medical Register and who has such experience or training in gynecology and obstetrics as may be prescribed by rules made under this Act.

3. When Pregnancies may be terminated by registered medical practitioners.-

(1) Notwithstanding anything contained in the Indian Penal Code (45 of 1860), a registered medical practitioner shall not be guilty of any offence under that Code or under any other law for the time being in force, if any pregnancy is terminated by him in accordance with the provisions of this Act.

(2) Subject to the provisions of sub-section (4), a pregnancy may be terminated by a registered medical practitioner,-

(a)where the length of the pregnancy does not exceed twelve weeks if such medical practitioner is,

or

101

(b)where the length of the pregnancy exceeds twelve weeks but does not exceed twenty weeks, if not less than two registered medical practitioners are.

Of opinion, formed in good faith, that,-

(i) the continuance of the pregnancy would involve a risk to the life of the pregnant woman or of grave injury physical or mental health ; or

(ii) there is a substantial risk that if the child were born, it would suffer from such physical or mental abnormalities as to be seriously handicapped.

Explanation 1.-Where any, pregnancy is alleged by the pregnant woman to have been caused by rape, the anguish caused by such pregnancy shall be presumed to constitute a grave injury to the mental health of the pregnant woman.

Explanation 2.-Where any pregnancy occurs as a result of failure of any device or method used by any married woman or her husband for the purpose of limiting the number of children, the anguish caused by such unwanted pregnancy may be presumed to constitute a grave injury to the mental health of the pregnant woman.

(3)In determining whether the continuance of pregnancy would involve such risk of injury to the health as is mentioned in sub-section (2), account may be taken of the pregnant woman's actual or reasonable foreseeable environment.

(4)(a) No pregnancy of a woman, who has not attained the age of eighteen years, or, who, having attained the age of eighteen years, is a lunatic, shall be terminated except with the consent in writing of her guardian.

(b)Save as otherwise provided in C1.(a), no pregnancy shall be terminated except with the consent of the pregnant woman.

4. Place where pregnancy may be terminated.-No termination of pregnancy shall be made in accordance with this Act at any place other than,-

(a)a hospital established or maintained by Government, or

(b)a place for the time being approved for the purpose of this Act by Government.

5. **Sections 3 and 4 when not to apply**.-

(1) The provisions of Sec.4 and so much of the provisions of sub-section (2 of Sec. 3 as relate to the length of the pregnancy and the opinion of not less than two registered medical practioner, shall not apply to the termination of a pregnancy by the registered medical practitioner in case where he is of opinion, formed in good faith, that the termination of such pregnancy is immediately necessary to save the life of the pregnant woman.

(2)Notwithstanding anything contained in the Indian Penal Code (45 of 1860), the termination of a pregnancy by a person who is not a registered medical practitioner shall be an offence punishable under that Code, and that Code shall, to this extent, stand modified.

6.**Power to make rules**.-4

(1)The Central Government may, by notification in the Official Gazette, make rules to carry out the provisions of

this Act.

(2)In particular, and without prejudice to the generality of the foregoing power, such rules may provide for all or

any of the following matters, namely:

(a)the experience or training, or both, which a registered medical practitioner shall have if he intends

to terminate any pregnancy under this Act ; and

(b)such other matters as are required to be or may be, provided by rules made under this Act.

(3)Every rule made by the Central Government under this Act shall be laid, as soon as may be after it is made,

before each House of Parliament while it is in session for a total period of thirty days which may be comprised in one session or in two successive sessions, and If, before the expiry of the session which it is so

laid or the session immediately following, both Houses agree in making any modification in the rule or both

Houses agree that the rule should not be made, the rule shall thereafter have effect only in such modified form

or be of no effect, as the case may be; so, however, that any

such modification or annulment shall be without

prejudice to the validity of anything previously done under

that rule. 7.**Power to make regulations**.-

(1)The State Government may, by regulations,-

(a)require any such opinion as is referred to in sub-section (2) of Sec. 3 to be certified by a

registered medical practitioner or practitioners concerned in such form and at such time as be

specified in such regulations, and the preservation or disposal of such certificates;

(b)require any registered medical practitioner, who terminates a pregnancy to give intimation of

such termination and such other information relating to the termination as maybe specified in

such regulations;

(c)prohibit the disclosure, except to such persons and for such purposes as may be specified in

such regulations, of intimations given or information furnished inpursuance of such regulations.

(2)The intimation given an the information furnished inpursuance of regulations made by virtue of C1.(b)of

Sub-section(1) of shall be given or furnished, as the case may be, to the Chief Medical Officer of the State..

(3)Any person who wilfully contravenes or wilfully fails to comply with the requirements of any regulation made

under sub-section (1) shall be liable to be punished with fine which may extend to one thousand rupees.

8.**Protection of action taken in good faith**.- No suit for other legal proceedings shall lie against any registered medical practitioner for any damage caused likely to be caused by anything which is in good faith done or intended to be done under this act.

THE IMMORAL TRAFFIC (PREVENTION) ACT, 1956

An Act to provide in pursuance of the International Convention signed at New York on the 9th day of May, 1950, for the prevention of immoral traffic.

Be it enacted by Parliament in the Seventh Year of the Republic of India as follows:

1. Short title, extent and commencement.—(1) This Act may be called The Immoral Traffic (Prevention) Act, 1956.

(2) It extends to the whole of India.

(3) This section shall come into force at once; and the remaining provisions of this come into force on such date as the Central Government may, by notification in the official Gazette, appoint.

2. Definitions.—In this Act. unless the context otherwise requires—

(a) "brothel" includes any house, room, conveyance or place, or any portion of any house, room, conveyance or place, which is used for purposes of sexual exploitation or abuse for the gain of another person or for the mutual gain of two or more prostitutes;

(aa) "child" means a person who has not completed the age of eighteen years;

(b)"corrective institution" means an institution, by whatever name called (being an institution established or licenced as such under Section 21), in which persons, who are in need of correction, may be detained under this

Act, and includes a shelter where under trials may be kept in pursuance of this Act;

(c)"magistrate" means a Magistrate specified in the second column of the Schedule as being competent to exercise the powers conferred by the section in which the expression occurs and which is specified in the first column of the Schedule;

(d)"prescribed" means prescribed by rules made under this Act;

(e)[1] [* * * * * *].

(f)"prostitution" means the sexual exploitation or abuse of persons for commercial purposes or for consideration in money or in any other kind, and the expression "prostitute" shall be construed accordingly;

(g)"protective home" means an institution, by whatever name called (being an institution established or licenced as such under Section 21), in which persons who are in need of care and protection, may be kept under this Act and where appropriate technically qualified persons, equipments and other facilities have been provided but does not include,—

(i)a shelter where undertrials may be kept in pursuance of this Act, or

(ii)a corrective institution;

(h)"public place" means any place intended for use by, or accessible to, the publicand includes any public conveyance;

(i)"special police officer"means a police officer appointed by or on behalf of the State Government to be in charge of police duties within a specified area for the purpose of this Act;

(j)"trafficking police officer" means a police officer appointed by the Central Government under sub- section (4) of Section 13.

2-A. Rule of construction regarding enactments not extending to Jammu and Kashmir .—Any reference in this Act to a law which is not in force in the State of Jammu and Kashmir shall in relation to that State, be construed as a reference to the corresponding law, if any, in force in that State.

3. Punishment for keeping a brothel or allowing premises to be used as a brothel.— (1) Any person who keeps or manages, or acts or assists in the keeping or management of, a brothel shall be punishable on first conviction with rigorous imprisonment for a term of not less than two years and which may extend to three years and also with fine which may extend to ten thousand rupees and in the event of a second or subsequent conviction, with rigorous imprisonment for a term which shall not be less than three

years and which may extend to seven years and shall also be liable to fine which may extend to two lakh rupees

(2) a any person who,—

(a)being the tenant, lessee, occupier or person in charge of any premises, uses, or knowingly allows any other person to use, such premises or any part thereof as a brothel, or

(b)being the owner, lessor or landlord of any premises or the agent of such owner, lessor or landlord, lets the same or any part thereof with the knowledge that the same or any part thereof is intended to be used as a brothel, or is wilfully a party to the use of such premises or any part thereof as a brothel,

shall be punishable on first conviction with imprisonment for a term which may extend to two years and with fine which fine which may extend to two thousand rupees and in the event of a second or subsequent conviction, with rigorous imprisonment for a term which may extend to five years and also with fine.

(2-A) For the purposes of sub-section (2), it shall be presumed, until the contrary is proved, that any person referred to in clause (a) or clause (b) of that sub-section, is knowingly allowing the premises or any part thereof to be used as a brothel or, as the case may be, has knowledge that the premises or any part thereof are being used as a brothel, if,—

(a)a report is published in a newspaper having circulation in the area in which such person resides to the effect that the premises or any part thereof have been found to be used for prostitution as a result of a search made under this Act; or

(b)a copy of the list of all things found during the search referred to in clause (a) is given to such person.

(3) Notwithstanding any thing contained in any other law for the time being in force, on conviction of any person referred to in clause (a) or clause (d) of sub-section (2) of any offence under that sub-section in respect of any premises or any part thereof, any lease or agreement under which such premises have been leased out or held or occupied at the time of the commission of the offence, shall become void and inoperative with effect from the date of the said conviction.

4. Punishment for living on the earnings of prostitution .—(1) Any person over the age of eighteen years who knowingly lives, wholly or in part, on

the earnings of the prostitution of any other person shall be punishable with imprisonment for a term which may extend to two years, or with fine which may extend to one thousand rupees, or with both, and where such earnings relate to the prostitution of a child, shall be punishable with imprisonment for a term of not less than seven years and not more than ten years.

(2) Where any person over the age of eighteen years is proved,—

(a)to be living with,or to be habitually in the company of, a prostitute; or

(b)to have exercised control, direction or influence over the movements of a prostitute in such a manner as to show that such person is aiding abetting or compelling her prostitution; or

(c)to be acting as a tout or pimp on behalf of a prostitute,

it shall be presumed, until the contrary is proved, that such person is knowingly living on the earnings of prostitution of another person within the meaning of sub-section (1).

5. Procuring, inducing or taking person for the sake of prostitution .—
(1) Any person who—

(a)procures or attempts to procure a person whether with or without his/her consent, for the purpose of prostitution; or

(b)induces a person to go from any place, with the intent that he/she may for the purpose of prostitution become the inmate of, or frequent, a brothel; or

(c)takes or attempts to take a person or causes a person to be taken, from one place to another with a view to his/her carrying on, or being brought up to carry on prostitution ; or

(d)causes or induces a person to carry on prostitution;

shall be punishable on conviction with rigorous imprisonment for a term of not less than three years and not more than seven years and also with fine which may extend to two thousand rupees, and if any offence under this sub-section is committed against the will of any person, the punishment of imprisonment for a term of seven years shall extend to imprisonment for a term of fourteen years:

Provided that if the person in respect of whom an offence committed under this subsection, is a child, the punishment provided under this sub-section shall extend to rigorous imprisonment for a term of not less than seven years but may extend to life

TRANSGENDER PROBLEMS AND TRANSGENDER.

Asian countries have centuries-old histories of existence of gender-variant males - who in present times would have been labelled as 'transgender women'. India is no exception. Kama Sutra provides vivid description of sexual life of people with 'third nature' (Tritiya Prakriti).

In India, people with a wide range of transgender-related identities, cultures, or experiences exist - including Hijras, Aravanis, Kothis, Jogtas/Jogappas, and Shiv-Shakthis (See glossary). Often these people have been part of the broader culture and treated with great respect, at least in the past, although some are still accorded particular respect even in the present.

The term 'transgender people' is generally used to describe those who transgress social gender norms. Transgender is often used as an umbrella term to signify individuals who defy rigid, binary gender constructions, and who express or present a breaking and/or blurring of culturally prevalent stereotypical gender roles. Transgender people may live full- or part-time in the gender role 'opposite' to their biological sex.

In contemporary usage, "transgender" has become an umbrella term that is used to describe a wide range of identities and experiences, including but not limited to: pre-operative, post-operative and non-operativetranssexual people (who strongly identify with the gender opposite to their biological sex); male and female'cross-dressers'(sometimes referred to as "transvestites", "drag queens", or "drag kings"); and men and women, regardless of sexual orientation, whose appearance or characteristics are perceived to be gender- atypical. A male-to-female transgender person is referred to as 'transgender woman' and a female-to-maletransgender person, as 'transgender man'.

The terms 'transgender' or 'transgender populations/people', used in this brief, while more encompassing than transgender women, are used to refer to transwomen given this brief's focus. Sometimes, for brevity, the abbreviation 'TG' is used to denote transgender women.

Until recently, HIV programs in India included transgender women under the epidemiological and behavioural term - 'men who have sex with men' (MSM), although many transgender people did not want to be included under that term. In addition to respecting the preferred term to be used by the transgender women, it is increasingly recognised that transgender people have unique needs and concerns, and that it is better to view them as a separate group that is not under the rubric of 'MSM'.

Even the umbrella term 'transgender' may hide the complexity and diversity of the various subgroups of gender-variant people in India and may hinder development of subgroup-specific HIV prevention and care interventions, and policies. For example, some Hijra activists may prefer others calling them 'Hijras' and not to subsume Hijras under the broader category 'transgender'. One reason for this is that they feel Hijras have a long history, culture and tradition in India, which would not be evident or which might be overlooked when using the catch-all term 'transgender'. Though some Hijra activists may also identify as 'transgender' for outsiders or in the global platform, they prefer the label 'transgender women' to be applied to those transgender women who are not part of the Hijra communities. However, some other Hijra/Aravani (Hijras in

Tamil Nadu) activists may identify as both 'Hijras/Aravanis' and 'transgender woman'.

Transgender people face multiple forms of oppression. The focus of this brief is to summarize the various issues faced by Hijras and transgender women by using the s

HIV AND HEALTH-RELATED RISKS

HIV and STI prevalence among transgender populations in India

The estimated size of MSM and male sex worker populations in India (latter presumably includes Hijras/TG communities) is 2,352,133 and 235,213, respectively. No reliable estimates are available for Hijras/TG women.

HIV prevalence among MSM populations was 7.4% as against the overall adult HIV prevalence of 0.36%. Until recently, Hijras/transgender people were included under the category of MSM in HIV sentinel serosurveillance. Recent studies among hijras/transgender (TG) women have indicated a very high HIV prevalence (17.5% to 41%) among them.

A study conducted in a Mumbai STI clinic reported very high HIV seroprevalence of 68% and high syphilis prevalence of 57% among Hijras. In Southern India, a study documented a high HIV seroprevalence (18.1%) and Syphilis prevalence (13.6%) among Hijras. A study conducted in Chennai documented high HIV and STI prevalence among Aravanis: 17.5% diagnosed positive for HIV and 72% had at least one STI (48% tested seropositive for HSV-1; 29% for HSV-2; and 7.8% for HBV).

Published data on sexual risk behaviours of Hijras/TG women are limited but available data indicate high risk sexual behaviors. The available information from the Integrated Biological and Behavioural Assessment (IBBA) survey 2007 conducted in select districts of Tamil Nadu, reported that, among Hijras/TG, the condom use during last anal sex with commercial male partners and 81% with non-commercial male partners is 85% and 81% respectively. Also, the survey documented low level of consistent condom use among Hijras/TG women: 6% with commercial male partners and 20% with non-commercial male partners.

Sexual health

Hijras/TG communities face several sexual health issues including HIV. Both personal- and contextual- level factors influence sexual health condition and access to and use of sexual health services. For example, most Hijras/TG are from lower socioeconomic status and have low literacy levels that pose barrier to seeking health care. Consequently, Hijras/TG communities face some unique barriers in accessing treatment services for STIs.

Mental health

Mental health needs of Hijras/TG communities are barely addressed in the current HIV programs. Some of the mental health issues reported in different community forums include depression and suicidal tendencies, possibly secondary to societal stigma, lack of social support, HIV status, and violence-related stress.

Most transgender people, especially youth, face great challenges in coming to terms with one's own gender identity and/or gender expression which are opposite to that of the gender identity and gender role imposed on them on the basis of their biological sex. They face several issues such as: shame, fear, and internalized transphobia; disclosure and coming out; adjusting, adapting, or not adapting to social pressure to conform; fear of relationships or loss of relationships; and self-imposed limitations on expression or aspirations.

TG Issue Brief, UNDP, VC. Dec. 2010

Alcohol and substance use

Available evidence suggest the need to address alcohol and substance use among Hijras/TG communities. An unknown but significant proportion of Hijras/TG communities consume alcohol possibly to forget stress and depression that they face in their daily life. Hijras provide several reasons justifying their alcohol consumption that range from the need to 'forget worries' (because there is no family support or no one cares about them) to managing rough clients in their sex work life. However, alcohol use is associated with inability to use condoms or insist their clients to use condoms, and thus increase risk for

HIV transmission and acquisition.

UNIT III:

Problems of children- destitution- physically and mentally challenged children-illiteracy-mallnutrition-maladjustmenting-childhood-child labour- the child prohibition and regulation act 1986-child marriage

restraint 1929-the juvenile justice act 2000- prohibition and regulation amendment act 1978.

PROBLEMS OF CHILDREN

Millions of children in today's world undergo the worst forms of child labor which includes Child Slavery, Child prostitution, Child Trafficking, Child Soldiers. In this modern era of material and technological advancement, children in almost every country are being callously exploited.

Child labor:

With an estimated 12.6 million children engaged in hazardous occupations (2001 Census India), our Country has the largest number of child labourers under the age of 14 in the world. Although poverty is often cited as the cause underlying child labour, other factors such as discrimination, social exclusion, as well as the lack of quality education, existing parents' attitudes and perceptions about child labour and the role and value of education need also to be considered. In states like Bihar, Mizoram, Rajasthan and Uttar Pradesh, 60 per cent or more girls are dropped out before completing their five years of primary education.

Why should we care?

Many children in hazardous and dangerous jobs are in danger of injury, even death.

In coming two decades, some millions of people will join the India's workforce. How many will have had to work at an early age, destroying their health or hampering their education?

Child Trafficking:

The nature and scope of trafficking range from industrial and domestic labour, to forced early marriages and commercial sexual exploitation. Existing studies show that over 40 per cent of women sex workers enter into prostitution before the age of 18 years. Moreover, for children who have been trafficked and rescued, opportunities for rehabilitation remains scarce and reintegration process arduous.

The worst sufferer among working children are those who are employed for household work and commonly referred as child domestic workers (CDWs). For a long time the official agencies responsible for protection of children denied their existence.

Our constitution prohibits human trafficking and successive governments have formulated laws intended to tackle it, with the primary legislative tool being the Immoral Traffic (Prevention) Act 1956. However these laws are either weak or inadequately enforced.

Children's vulnerability and exposure to violations of their rights remains widespread and multiple in nature. But the real cause of worry is UNIFEM's report which says s that 40 % of India's police officers are unaware of child trafficking problem.

But due to constant campaign by the NGOs supported by international agencies (such as Misereor, Bread for the World, Christian Aid, Oxfam, CIDA, Novib, Caritas, CRS, DANIDA etc.) , now the Government has banned employment of children's below 14 years as domestic help from 10 th October 2006.It is reported that in Metropolitan cities like Mumbai, Kolkatta, Delhi and Chennai majority of domestic help are children particularly girls below 14 years.

Infant Mortality:

Infant mortality is as high as 63 deaths per 1,000 live births. Most infant deaths occur in the first month of life; up to 47 per cent in the first week itself. While the Infant Mortality Rate showed a rapid decline during the 1980s, the decrease has slowed during the past decade. Maternal deaths are similarly high.

The reasons for this high mortality are that few women have access to skilled birth attendants and fewer still to quality emergency obstetric care. In addition, only 15 per cent of mothers receive complete antenatal care and only 58 per cent receive iron or folate tablets or syrup.

HIV /AIDS

Its is estimated 220,000 children infected by HIV/AIDS and 55,000 to 60,000 children are born every year to mothers who are HIV positive. Without treatment, these newborns stand an estimated 30% chance of becoming infected during the mother's pregnancy, labor or through breastfeeding after six months. There is effective treatment available, but this is not reaching all women and children who need it.

The mobilization and greater involvement of NGOs in programmes for the development of children and women has increased the potential to accelerate the development process in achieving the national goals for children.

Other issues:

- Polio remains a serious threat, notwithstanding a massive campaign to eradicate it. Children continue to die of vaccine-preventable diseases such as measles.
- Malnutrition affects nearly half of all children under age five.

THE CHILD LABOUR (PROHIBITION AND REGULATION) ACT, 1986

(ACT NO. 61 OF 1986)

[23rd December, 1986.]

An Act to prohibit the engagement of children in certain employments and to regulate the conditions of work of children in certain other employments.

Be it enacted by Parliament in the Thirty-Seventh Year of the Republic of India as follows: --

PART I

PRELIMINARY

1. Short title, extent and commencement. -- (1) This Act may be called the Child Labour (Prohibition and Regulation) Act, 1986.

(2)It extends to the whole of India.

(3)The provisions of this Act, other than Part III, shall come into force at once, and Part III shall come into force on such date as the Central Government may, by notification in the Official Gazette, appoint, and different dates may be appointed for different States and for different classes of establishments.

2. Definitions. -- In this Act, unless the context otherwise requires, --

(i) "appropriate Government" means, in relation to an establishment under the control of the Central Government or a railway administration or a major port or a mine or oilfield, the Central Government, and in all other cases, the State Government;

(ii)"child" means a person who has not completed his fourteenth year of age;

(iii)"day" means a period of twenty-four hours beginning at mid-night;

(iv) "establishment" includes a shop, commercial establishment, workshop,

> farm, residential hotel, restaurant, eating house, theatre or other place of amusemen
> public t   or entertainment;

(v) "family", in relation to an occupier, means the individual, the wife or husband, as the case may be, of such individual, and their children, brother or sister of such individual;

(vi) "occupier", in relation to an establishment or a workshop, means the person who has the ultimate control over the affairs of the establishment or workshop;

(vii)"port authority" means any authority administering a port;

(viii)"prescribed" means prescribed by rules made under section 18, (ix)"week" means a period of seven days beginning at midnight on Saturday night or such other night as may be approved in writing for a particular area by the Inspector;

(x)"workshop" means any premises (including the precincts thereof) wherein any industrial process is carried on, but does not include any premises to which the provisions of section 67 of the Factories Act, 1948 (63 of 1948), for the time being, apply.

PART II

PROHIBITION OF EMPLOYMENT OF CHILDREN IN CERTAIN OCCUPATIONS AND PROCESSES

3. Prohibition of employment of children in certain occupations andprocesses.-- No child shall be employed or permitted to work in any of the occupations set forth in Part A of the Schedule or in any workshop wherein any of the processes set forth in Part B of the Schedule is carried on:

Provided that nothing in this section shall apply to any workshop wherein any process is carried on by the occupier with the aid of his family or to any school established by, or receiving assistance or recognition from, Government.

4. Power to amend the Schedule.-- The Central Government, after giving by notification in the Official Gazette, not less than three months notice of its intention so to do, may, by like notification, add any occupation or process to the Schedule and thereupon the Schedule shall be deemed to have been amended accordingly.

5. *Child Labour Technical Advisory Committee.--* (1) The Central Government may, by notification in the Official Gazette, constitute an advisory committee to be called the Child Labour Technical Advisory Committee (hereafter in this section referred to as the

Committee) to advise the Central Government for the purpose of addition of occupations and processes to the Schedule.

(2) The Committee shall consist of a Chairman and such other members not exceeding ten, as may be appointed by the Central Government.

(3)The Committee shall meet as often as it may consider necessary and shall have power to regulate its own procedure.

(4)The Committee may, if it deems it necessary so to do, constitute one or more
sub-committees and may appoint to any such sub-committee, whether generally or for the consideration of any particular matter, any person who is not a member of the Committee.

(5) The term of office, of the manner of filling casual vacancies in the office of, and the allowances, if any, payable to, the Chairman and other members of the Committee, and the conditions and restrictions subject to which the Committee may appoint any person who is not a member of the Committee as a member of any of its sub- committees shall be such as may be prescribed.

PART III

REGULATION OF CONDITIONS OF WORK OF CHILDREN

6.Application of Part.-- The provisions of this Part shall apply to an establishment or a class of establishments in which none of the occupations or processes referred to in section 3 is carried on.

7.Hours and period of work. -- (1) No child shall be required or permitted to work in any establishment in excess of such number of hours as may be prescribed for such establishment or class of establishments.

(2) The period of work on each day shall be so fixed that no period shall exceed three hours and that no child shall work for more than three hours before he has had an interval for rest for at least one hour.

(4)No child shall be permitted or required to work between 7 p.m. and 8 a.m.

(5)No child shall be required or permitted to work overtime.

8. Weekly holidays.-- Every child employed in an establishment shall be allowed in each week, a holiday of one whole day, which day shall be specified by the occupier in a notice permanently exhibited in a conspicuous place in the establishment and the day so specified shall not be altered by the occupier more than once in three months.

9. Notice to Inspector.-- (1) Every occupier in relation to an establishment in which a child was employed or permitted to work immediately before the date of commencement of this Act in relation to such establishment shall, within a period of thirty days from such commencement, send to the Inspector within whose local limits the establishment is situated, a written notice containing the following particulars,namely:--

(a) the name and situation of the establishment;

(b) the name of the person in actual management of the establishment;

(c) the address to which communications relating to the establishment should be sent; and

(d)the nature of the occupation or process carried on in the establishment.

(2)Every occupier, in relation to an establishment, who employs, or permits to work, any child after the date of commencement of this Act in relation to such establishment, shall, within a period of thirty days from the date of such employment, send to the Inspector within whose local limits the establishment is situated, a written notice containing the particulars as are mentioned in sub-section (1).

Explanation.-- For the purposes of sub-sections (1) and (2), "date of commencement of this Act, in relation to an establishment" means the date of bringing into force of this Act in relation to such establishment.

(a)the name and date of birth of every child so employed or permitted to work;

(b)hours and periods of work of any such child and the intervals of rest to which he is entitled;

(c)the nature of work of any such child; and

(d)such other particulars as may be prescribed.

12.Display of notice containing abstract of sections 3 and 14.-- Every railway administration, every port authority and every occupier shall cause to be displayed in a conspicuous and accessible place at every station on its railway or within the limits of a port or at the place of work, as the case may be, a notice in the local language and in the English language containing an abstract of sections 3 and 14.

13.Health and safety.-- (1) The appropriate Government may, by notification in the

Official Gazette, make rules for the health and safety of the children employed or permitted to work in any establishment or class of establishments.

(2) Without prejudice to the generality of the foregoing provisions, the said rules may provide for all or any of the following matters, namely:--

(a)cleanliness in the place of work and its freedom from nuisance;

(b)disposal of wastes and effluents;

(c)ventilation and temperature;

(d)dust and fume;

(e)artificial humidification;

(f)lighting;

(g)drinking water;

(h)latrine and urinals;

(i)spittoons;

(j)fencing of machinery;

(k)work at or near machinery in motion;

(l)employment of children on dangerous machines;

(m)instructions, training and supervision in relation to employment of children on dangerous machines;

(n)device for cutting off power;

(o)self-acting machines;

(p)easing of new machinery;

(q)floor, stairs and means of access;

(r)pits, sumps, openings in floors, etc.;

(s)excessive weights;

(t)protection of eyes;

(u)explosive or inflammable dust, gas, etc.;

(v)precautions in case of fire;

(w)maintenance of buildings; and

(x)safety of buildings and machinery.

PART IV

MISCELLANEOUS

14. Penalties.-- (1) Whoever employs any child or permits any child to work in contravention of the provisions of section 3 shall be punishable with imprisonment for a term which shall not be less than three months but which may extend to one year or with fine which shall not be less than ten thousand rupees but which may extend to twenty thousand rupees or with both.

(2) Whoever, having been convicted of an offence under section 3, commits a like offence afterwards, he shall be punishable with imprisonment for a term which shall not be less than six months but which may extend to two years

The Child Marriage Restraint Act, 1929
(19 of 1929)
An Act to restrain the solemnisation of child marriage.
Section 1 : Short title extent and commencement --
   (1) This Act may be called the Child Marriage Restraint Act, (1929).
         (2) It extends to the whole of India (except the State of Jammu and Kashmir) and it applies also to all citizen of India without and beyond India.
         (3) It shall come into force on the 1st day of April, 1930.
Section 2 : Definitions -- In this Act, unless there is anything repugnant   in the subject or context:
         (a) "Child" means a person who, if a male, has not completed twenty one year of age, and if a female, has not completed eighteen years of age ;
         (b) "child marriage" means a marriage to which either of the contracting parties is a child ;
         (c) "contracting party" to a marriage means either of the parties whose marriage is (or is about to be) thereby solemnised and
         (d) "minor" means a person of either sex who is under eighteen years of age.
Section 3 : Punishment for male adult below twenty one years of age marrying a child -- Whoever, being a male above eighteen years of age and below twenty one, contracts a child marriage shall be punishable with

simple imprisonment which may extend to fifteen days, or with fine which may extend to one thousand rupees, or with both .

Section 4 : Punishment for male adult above twenty one years of age marrying a child -- Whoever, being a male above twenty one years of age, contracts a child marriage shall be punishable with simple imprisonment which may extend to three months and shall also be liable to fine.

Section 5 : Punishment for solemnising a child marriage -- (1) Whoever performs, conducts or directs any child marriage shall be punishable with simple imprisonment which may extend to three months and shall also be liable to fine unless he proves that he had reason to believe that the marriage was not a child -marriage.

Section 6   Punishment for parent or guardian concerned in a child marriage --

(1) Where a minor contracts a child marriage, any person having charge of the minor, whether as parent or guardian or in any other capacity, lawful or unlawful, who does any act to promote the marriage or permits it to be solemnised, or negligently fails to prevent it from being solemnised, shall be punishable with simple imprisonment which may extend to three months and shall also be liable to fine.

Provided no woman shall be punishable with imprisonment.

(2) For the purpose of this section, it shall be presumed unless and until the contrary is proved, that where a minor has contracted a child marriage, the person having charge of such minor has negligently failed to prevent marriage from being solemnised.

Section 7 : Offences to be cognizable for certain purposes. The Code of Criminal Procedure, 1973 (2 of 1974) shall apply to offences under this Act as if they were cognizable offences -

(a) for the purpose of investigation of such offences : and

(b) for the purposes of matters other than (i) matters referred to in Section 42 of that Code and (ii) the arrest of a person without a warrant or without an order of a Magistrate.

Section 8 : Jurisdiction under this Act - Notwithstanding anything contained in Section 190 of the (Code of Criminal Procedure, 1973) (2 of 1974), no Court other than that of a Metropolitan Magistrate or a Judicial Magistrate of the first class shall take cognizance of, or try, any offence under this Act.

Section 9 : Mode of taking cognizance of offences -- No Court shall take cognizance of any offence under this Act after the expiry of one year from the date on which the offence is alleged to have been   committed.

Section 10 : Preliminary inquiries into offences -- Any Court, on receipt of a complaint of an offence of which it is authorised to take cognizance, shall unless it dismisses the complaint under Section 203 of the Code of Criminal Procedure, 1973 (2 of 1974) either itself make an inquiry under Section 202 of that Code or direct a Magistrate subordinate to it to make such inquiry.

Section 11 -- Repealed by the Child Marriage Restraint (Amendment) Act, 1949 (41 of 1949), Section 7.

Section 12 : Power to issue injunction prohibiting marriage in contravention of this Act --

> (1) Notwithstanding anything to the contrary contained in this Act the Court may, if satisfied from information laid before it through a complaint or otherwise that a child marriage in contravention of this Act has been arranged or is about to be solemnised, issue an injunction against any of the persons mentioned in Sections 3, 4, 5 and 6 of this Act prohibiting such marriage.

> (2) No injunction under sub-section (1) shall be issued against any person unless the Court has previously given notice to such person, and has afforded him an opportunity to show cause against the issue of the injunction.

> (3) The Court may either on its own motion or on the application of any person aggrieved rescind or alter any order made under sub-section (1).

> (4) Where such an application is received, the Court shall afford the applicant an early, opportunity of appearing before it either in person or by pleader, and if the Court rejects the application wholly or in part, it shall record in writing its reasons for so doing.

> (5) Whoever knowing that an injunction has been issued against him under sub-section (1) of this Section disobeys, such injunction shall be punished with imprisonment or either description for a term which may extend to three months, or with fine which may extend to one thousand rupees, or with both.

Provided that no woman shall be punishable with imprisonment.

THE JUVENILE JUSTICE ACT 2000

PRELIMINARY

1.Short title and commencement.— (1) These rules may be called the Juvenile Justice (Care and Protection of Children) Rules, 2007.

(2)They shall come into force on the date of their publication in the Official Gazette.

2.Definition.—In these rules, unless the context otherwise requires-

(a)"abandoned" means an unaccompanied and deserted child who is declared abandoned by the Committee after due inquiry;

(b)"Act" means the Juvenile Justice (Care and Protection of Children) Act, 2000 (56 of 2000) as amended by the Juvenile Justice (Care and Protection of Children) Amendment Act, 2006 (33 of 2006);

(c)"best interest of the child" means a decision taken to ensure the physical, emotional, intellectual, social and moral development of juvenile or child;

(d)"child friendly" means any process and interpretation, attitude, environment and treatment, that is humane, considerate and in the best interest of the child;

(e)"community service" implies service rendered to the society by juveniles in conflict with law in lieu of other judicial remedies and penalties, which is not degrading and dehumanizing. Examples of this may include:

(i)cleaning a park;

(ii)getting involved with Habitat for Humanity;

(iii)serving the elderly in nursing homes;

(iv)helping out a local fire or police department;

(v)helping out at a local hospital or nursing home; and

(vi)serving disabled children.

(f) "detention" in case of juveniles in conflict with law means "protective custody" in line with the principles of restorative justice;

(g)"Form" means the form annexed to these rules;

(h)"individual care plan" is a comprehensive development plan for a juvenile or child based on age specific and gender specific needs and the case history of the juvenile or child, prepared in consultation with the juvenile or child, in order to restore the juvenile's or child's self-esteem, dignity and self-worthand nurture him into a responsible citizen and accordingly the plan shall address the following needs of a juvenile or a child:

(i)Health needs;

(ii)Emotional and psychological needs;

(iii)Educational and training needs;

(iv)Leisure, creativity and play;

(v)Attachments and relationships;

(vi)Protection from all kinds of abuse, neglect and maltreatment;

(vii)Social mainstreaming; and

(viii)Follow-up post release and restoration.

(i)"institution" means an observation home, or a special home, or a children's home or a shelter home set up, certified or recognized and registered under sections 8, 9, 34, sub-section (3) of section 34 and section 37 of the Act respectively;

(j)"Officer-in-charge" or such other nomenclature as issued by the State Government, means a person appointed for the control and management of the institution;

(k)"orphan" means a child who is without parents or willing and capable legal or natural guardian;

(l)"place of safety" means any institution set up and recognized under sub-section (3) of section 12 andsub-section (1) of section 16 of the Act for juvenile in conflict with law or children;

(m)"recognised" means a person found fit by the competent authority or, an institution found fit by the State Government on the recommendation of the competent authority as per clauses (h) and (i) of section (2) of the Act; or, recognition of an institution or agency or voluntary organisation by the State Government to operate as a children's home, observation home and special home; or a shelter home, specialised adoption agency or after care organization under sub-section (1) of section 37, sub-section(4) of section 41 and clause (a) of section 44 of the Act;

(n)"registered" means all institutions or agencies or voluntary organisations providing residential care to children in need of care and protection registered under sub-section (3) of section 34;

(o)"State Government" in relation to a Union Territory means the Administrator of that Union Territory appointed by the President under article 239 of the Constitution;

(p)"street and working children" means children without ostensible means of livelihood, care, protection and support in accordance with the provisions laid down under clause (d) (1) of section 2 of the Act;

(q)"surrendered child" means a child, who in the opinion of the Committee, is relinquished on account of physical, emotional and social factors beyond the control of the parent or guardian;

(r)all words and expressions defined in the Act and used, but not defined in these rules, shall have the same meaning as assigned to them in the Act.

CHAPTER - II

FUNDAMENTAL PRINCIPLES OF JUVENILE JUSTICE AND PROTECTION OF CHILDREN

3. Fundamental principles to be followed in administration of these rules — (1) The State Government, the Juvenile Justice Board, the Child Welfare Committee or other competent authorities or agencies, as the case may be, while implementing the provisions of these rules shall abide and be guided by the principles, specified in sub-rule (2).

(2) The following principles shall, *interalia,* be fundamental to the application, interpretation and implementation of the Act and the rules made hereunder:

I. Principle of presumption of innocence:

(a)A juvenile or child or juvenile in conflict with law is presumed to be innocent of any malafide or criminal intent up to the age of eighteen years.

(b)The juvenile's or juvenile's in conflict with law or child's right to presumption of innocence shall be respected throughout the process of justice and protection, from the initial contact to alternative care, including aftercare.

(c)Any unlawful conduct of a juvenile or a child or a juvenile in conflict with law which is done for survival, or is due to environmental or situational factors or is done under control of adults, or peer groups, is ought to be covered by the principles of innocence.

(d)The basic components of presumption of innocence are:

(i) Age of innocence

Age of innocence is the age below which a juvenile or child or a juvenile in conflict with law cannot be subjected to the criminal justice system. The Beijing Rule 4(1) clearly lays down that "the beginning of the age of criminal responsibility shall not be fixed at too low an age level bearing in mind the facts of mental and intellectual maturity". In consonance with this principle, the mental and intellectual maturity of juvenile or child or a juvenile in conflict with law below eighteen years is considered insufficient through out the world.

(ii) Procedural protection of innocence

All procedural safeguards that are guaranteed by the Constitution and other statutes to the adults and that go in to strengthen the juvenile's or child's right to presumption of innocence **shall be guaranteed to juveniles or the children or juveniles in conflict with law.**

(iii) Provisions of Legal aid and Guardian Ad Litem

Juveniles in conflict with law have a right to be informed about the accusations against them and a right to be legally represented. Provisions must be made for guardian ad litem, legal aid and other such assistance through legal services at State expense. This shall also include such juveniles right to present his case before the competent authority on his own.

II Principle of dignity and worth:

(a)Treatment that is consistent with the child's sense of dignity and worth is a fundamental principle of juvenile justice. This principle reflects the fundamental human right enshrined in Article 1 of the Universal Declaration of Human Rights that all human beings are born free and equal in dignity and rights. Respect of dignity includes not being humiliated, personal identity, boundaries and space being respected, not being labeled and stigmatized, being offered information and choices and not being blamed for their acts.

(b)The juvenile's or child's right to dignity and worth has to be respected and protected throughout the entire process of dealing with the child from the first contact with law enforcement agencies to the implementation of all measures for dealing with the child.

III. Principle of Right to be heard:

Every child's right to express his views freely in all matters affecting his interest shall be fully respected through every stage in the process of juvenile justice. Children's right to be heard shall include creation of developmentally appropriate tools and processes of interacting with the child, promoting children's active involvement in decisions regarding their own lives and providing opportunities for discussion and debate.

IV. Principle of Best Interest:

(a)In all decisions taken within the context of administration of juvenile justice, the principle of best interest of the juvenile or the juvenile in conflict with law or child shall be the primary consideration.

(b)The principle of best interest of the juvenile or juvenile in conflict with law or child shall mean for instance that the traditional objectives of criminal justice, retribution and repression, must give way to rehabilitative and restorative objectives of juvenile justice.

 (c) This principle seeks to ensure physical, emotional, intellectual, social and moral development of a juvenile in conflict with law or child so as to ensure the safety, well being and permanence for each child and thus enable each child to survive and reach his or her full potential.

V. Principle of family responsibility:

(a)The primary responsibility of bringing up children, providing care, support and protection shall be with the biological parents. However, in exceptional situations, this responsibility may be bestowed on willing adoptive or foster parents.

(b)All decision making for the child should involve the family of origin unless it is not in the best interest of the child to do so.

(c)The family - biological, adoptive or foster (in that order), must be held responsible and provide necessary care, support and protection to the juvenile or child under their care and custody under the Act, unless the best interest measures or mandates dictate otherwise.

VI. Principle of Safety (no harm, no abuse, no neglect, no exploitation and no maltreatment):

(a)At all stages, from the initial contact till such time he remains in contact with the care and protection system, and thereafter, the juvenile or child or juvenile in conflict with law shall not be subjected to any harm, abuse, neglect, maltreatment, corporal punishment or solitary or otherwise any confinement in jails and extreme care shall be taken to avoid any harm to the sensitivity of the juvenile or the child.

(b)The state has a greater responsibility for ensuring safety of every child in its care and protection, without resorting to restrictive measures and processes in the name of care and protection.

VII. Positive measures:

(a)Provisions must be made to enable positive measures that involve the full mobilization of all possible resources, including the family, volunteers and other community groups, as well as schools and other mainstream community institutions or processes, for the purpose of promoting the well-being of the juvenile or child through individual care plans carefully worked out.

(b)The positive measures shall aim at reducing vulnerabilities and reducing the need for intervention under the law, as well as effective, fair and humane dealing of the juvenile or child.

(c)The positive measures shall include avenues for health, education, relationships, livelihoods, leisure, creativity and play.

(d)Such positive measures must facilitate the development of identity for the child and provide them with an inclusive and enabling environment.

VIII. Principle of non-stigmatizing semantics, decisions and actions:

The non-stigmatizing semantics of the Act must be strictly adhered to, and the use of adversarial or accusatory words, such as, arrest, remand, accused, charge sheet, trial, prosecution, warrant, summons, conviction, inmate, delinquent, neglected, custody or jail is prohibited in the processes pertaining to the child or juvenile in conflict with law under the Act.

IX. Principle of non-waiver of rights:

(a)No waiver of rights of the child or juvenile in conflict with law, whether by himself or the competent authority or anyone acting or claiming to act on behalf of the juvenile or child, is either permissible or valid.

(b)Non-exercise of a fundamental right does not amount to waiver

X. Principle of equality and non-discrimination:

(a) There shall be no discrimination against a child or juvenile in conflict with law on the basis of age, sex, place of birth, disability, health, status, race, ethnicity, religion, caste, cultural practices, work, activity or behaviour of the juvenile or child or that of his parents or guardians, or the civil and political status of the juvenile or child.

(b)Equality of access, equality of opportunity, equality in treatment under the Act shall be guaranteed to every child or juvenile in conflict with law.

XI. Principle of right to privacy and confidentiality:

The juvenile's or child's right to privacy and confidentiality shall be protected by all means and through all the stages of the proceedings and care and protection processes.

XII. Principle of last resort:

Institutionalization of a child or juvenile in conflict with law shall be a step of the last resort after reasonable inquiry and that too for the minimum possible duration.

XIII. Principle of repatriation and restoration:

Every juvenile or child or juvenile in conflict with law has the right to be re-united with his family and restored back to the same socio-economic and cultural status that such juvenile or child enjoyed before coming within the purview of the Act or becoming vulnerable to any form of neglect, abuse or exploitation.

Any juvenile or child, who has lost contact with his family, shall be eligible for protection under the Act and shall be repatriated and restored, at the earliest, to his family, unless such repatriation and restoration is likely to be against the best interest of the juvenile or the child.

XIV. Principle of Fresh Start:

(a)The principle of fresh start promotes new beginning for the child or juvenile in conflict with law by ensuring erasure of his past records.

(b)The State shall seek to promote measures for dealing with children alleged or recognized as having impinged the penal law, without resorting to judicial proceedings

UNIT IV:

Problems of youth-youth policy and youth problem-problem of aged-causes and effect-problem of SC and ST -untouchablity-the protection of civil rights act 1955-the SC and ST prevention of atrocities act 1989-persones with disability (equal opportunity, protection of civil rights) full protection act 1995.

PROBLEMS OF YOUTH

The perennial task of man is to remake his world. But the world really belongs to the youth. The youth gives the hero and the followers who change the world from age to age. But it is an enigma that the youth does not remain young. He comes of age and is about to compromise with the world as it is. The youth of yesteryear engages himself in 'useful' works and forgets the 'noble deeds' which he did and dreamt of as a youth.

Time flows. History moves on. The 'gap' yawns as ever.

Today's youth is as restive, impatient with hypocrisy of the past and the dichotomy between precept and practice, and as stout a protagonist of recognition of his and others' identities, as was the youth of the time when Christ was not but Socrates was and commented on the youths. Because of the fleeting nature of youth, the young plunge into action before they could afford to plan something to achieve a well-chosen aim which would remove the incongruities which appeared intolerable to them.

The Problem

They have great enthusiasm, vigour, and will to remove ills and injustice in society, love and respect for ideals and values no yet defined or identified; their hopeful disposition makes them think themselves equal to

135

the great problems as they view them. In spite of all their qualities, enthusiasm, and will youths often fail in their mission and wait to see the same with youths of the future. What is the cause? As Aristotle put it: 'All their mistakes are in the direction of doing things excessively and vehemently. They overdo everything - they love too much, hate too much, and do the same with everything else.' This is inherent in the youth. This is their power and his again robs them of their real power. This is an enigma.

This may be called the style of the youth. This characteristic of the youth is Apparent in a small section which is active makes the style of the youth apparent and its existence felt. The characteristic of the young generation is the way they approach the world, the style of their action rather than ideologies or definite goals , to focus on the process rather than definite programmes, where 'flux is more obvious than fixed purpose.' The youths love to be 'psychologically open to a historically unpredictable future.' They abhor fixity, stability, and 'closedness' and prefer unfinishedness, flexibility, and openness. All this is good. But the trouble brews from the apparent idealization of such notions. It is good to start with flexibility and openness, but it is horrible to worship 'unfinishedness' all the time. The inherent desire of the youth for recognition and undefined identity involves, without their recognizing and admitting this, some sort of fixity, stability, and closedness. Without a fixed purpose, a goal, a programme, the vision of personal and collective future will ever remained blurred and vague.

In most cases this openness, this flexibility, this deliberate lack of a fixed purpose and goal, this want of a clear-cut long-range plan of action spills over to adulthood with the result that as adults we become the unwilling target of the new young generation. As with our once-cherished 'unfinishedness' still lingering with us we remain unequal to the great task of moulding our world and are accused of captaining a rudderless ship of society which brings to relief 'poverty in the midst of affluence, hypocrisy in stating one set of values and following another, rhetoric instead of action, promises without fulfillment, empty words.'

The new young generation revolts against all these, hates these too much, loves too much openness, flexibility, and lack of purpose, goal, programme and acts excessively and vehemently for some time until they tell apart 'noble deeds' and 'useful work', and become tired and unnoticed, when they reach adulthood, wait for a newer generation to curse them. This is almost an eternal problem with youth and unless something is and can be done about it youth problem will ever remain as illusive as it seems now.

Secondary Problems

All other problems of the youth are superficial and can be rather easily taken care of for solution till newer smaller problems pose for our attention. There are, however, some other problems of somewhat basic nature, which needs tackling for solution of the most vital problem of the youth discussed above. Basic problems pertaining to anything Superficial or secondary problems arise out of the reaction of the thing to actions of other things or environment. Such problems can be tackled by readjusting the actions of outer things or environments which is rather of an easier nature compared to dealing with basic problems coming from inner nature. Who does not know the secondary problems faced by the youth today? They don't have – many of them – proper nutrition, health care, amenities for proper development of their body and mind, scope for self-expression and cultural development, proper educational facilities, cheap text books, healthy reading materials, constructivemass-media, suitable accommodation for living, study, and recreation, employment opportunity, occupation suiting aptitudes, enough constructive work to keep them engaged in idle hours, etc. etc. These are more or less on the physical side and may be tackled externally if there is will. There are certain other secondary problems of the youth which are of mental or moral nature. Such as recognition of the youth, valuing their opinion, entrusting responsibility on them etc. These may also be tackled with understanding, sympathy, and will to use the youth potential.

But basic problems need deeper probe and demand subtle tackling where external methods have very little to do except by way of suggestions. Here the individual has to act internally to tackle the inner cause of the problem.

YOUTH PROBLEMS YOUTH POLICY YOUTH PROGRAMMES

YOUTH DEFINITION

- ☐ Youth means every person between the ages of **15** and **35** years.

- ☐ Youth is best understood as aeriod of transition from the dependence of childhood.

- ☐ Adulthoods independence and awareness of our interdependence as member of a community.

YOUTH PROGRAMMES

- ☐ Around one lakh Yuvak Manadals in rural areas organized under the community development progaramme.

- ☐ NSS in colleges and universities.

- ☐ Nehru Yuvak Kendra's at the district level for student and non-student youth.

- National graduate volunteer scheme.

- National Cadet Corps in colleges.

- Youth clubs organize by agricultural colleges, universities & training centers on community development.

NEEDS OF THE YOUTH

- To affect an integration in personality for becoming a mature and responsible adult.

- Outgrowing protection and developing emotional independence.

- To bring about necessary adjustment with opposite sex and achieving mature relation with age-mates and to prepare for family life.

- To select and prepare for a vocation in order to achieve economic independence.

YOUTH PROBLEMS

- To development in economic problems.

- To achievements can't reached to society.

- Affected to youth personal life.

- To development with out supports

PROBLEMS OF AGED

Aging

Problem of aging is an important problem of all times.

Those who are senior citizens of above the age of 50 - 65 are regarded as the aged.

It is the social welfare and social defense departments of the Government of India and many voluntary organizations that take care of the aged.

- Psychological Problems

    - Abandonment from families make the elderly people suffer from psychological stress

    - Depression due to the thought that they are going to die

    - The stress that arise due to the loss of their spouse, either male or female

    - Most of the elderly people suffer from mental impairment and memory loss

    - They suffer from depression due to the ill behaviour of their children

    - Emotional illness

    - Sadness without any reasons

    - Anxiety

    - Loneliness

    - Limited financial resources

    - Lower income

    - Lower social status

    - Non-acceptance of aging

- Health Related Problems

    - The elderly people are seen to suffer from many diseases

- They are likely to suffer from

  - Insomnia

  - Memory loss

  - Energy loss

  - Falling eye sight

  - Hearing loss

  - Heart problems

  - Neurotic problems

  - Stroke

  - Dementia

  - Obesity due to depression

  - Lower level of eating habits in some individuals

  - Paralysis

THE PROTECTION OF CIVIL RIGHTS ACT, 1955

Act, No.22 OF 1955) (As on the 1st September, 1977)

An Act to prescribe punishment for the preaching and practice of "untouchability" for the enforcement of any disability arising there from and for matters connected therewith. Be it enacted by Parliament in the Sixth Year of the Republic of India as follows:

1 Short Title, extent and commencement

(1)This Act may be called the Protection of Civil Rights Act,1955.

(2)It extends to the whole of India.

(3)It shall come into force on such date as the Central Government may, by notifications in the Official Gazette appoint.

2. Definitions

In this Act, unless the context otherwise requires:-

(a)   "civil rights" means any right accruing to a person by reason of the abolition of "untouchability" by article 17 of the Constitution;

(aa)   "hotel" includes a refreshment room, a boarding house, a lodging house, a coffee house and a café;

(b)   "place" includes a house, building and other structure and premises; and also includes a tent, vehicle and vessel;)

(c) "Place of public entertainment" includes any place to which the public are admitted and in which an entertainment is provided or held.

Explanation"-   "Entertainment"   includes   any   exhibition, performance, game, sport and other form of amusement;

(d)   "place of public worship" means a place, by whatever name known, which is used as a place of public religious worship or which is dedicated generally to, or is used generally by, persons professing any religion or belonging to any religious denomination or any section thereof, for the performance of any religious service, or for offering prayers therein; and includes-

(i)   all lands and subsidiary shrines appurtenant attached or to any such place;

(ii)   a privately owned place of worship which is, in fact, allowed by the owner thereof to be used as a place of public worship, and

(iii)   such land or subsidiary shrine appurtenant to such privately owned place of worship as is allowed by the owner thereof to be used as a place of public religious worship;)

(da)   "prescribed" means prescribed by rules made under this Act;

(db)   "scheduled castes" has the meaning assigned to it in clause (24) of article 366 of the Constitution;)

(e)   "shop" means any premises where goods are sold either wholesale or by retail or both wholesale and by retail and includes-

(i)   any place from where goods are sold by a hawker or vendor or from a mobile van or cart,

(ii)   a laundry and a hair cutting saloon;

(iii)   any other place where services are rendered to customers.

3. Punishments for enforcing religious disabilities

Whoever on the ground of "untouchability" prevents any person-

(a)   from entering any place of public worship which is open to other persons professing the same religion or any section thereof, as such person; or

(b)   from worshipping or offering prayers or performing any religious service in any place of public worship, or bathing or using the waters of, any sacred tank, well, spring or water-course (river or lake or bathing at any ghat of such tank, water-course, river or lake) in the same manner and to the same extent as is permissible to other persons professing the same religion or any section thereof, as such person;

shall be punishable imprisonment for a term of not less than one month and not more than six months and also with fine which shall be not less than one hundred rupees and not more than five hundred rupees.

Explanation- For the purpose of this section and section 4 persons professing the buddhist, Sikh or Jain religion or persons professing the Hindu religion in any of its forms or development including Virashaivas, Lingayats, Adivasis, followers of Brahmo, Prarthana, Arya Samaj and the Swaminarayan Sampraday shall be deemed to be Hindus.

4. Punishment for enforcing social disabilities

Whoever o the ground of "untouchability" enforces against any person any disability with regard to-

(i)   access to any shop, public restaurant, hotel or place of public entertainment; or

(ii)   the use of any utensils, and other articles kept in any public restaurant, hotel, dharmshala, sarai or musafirkhana for the use of the general public or of any section thereof; or

(iii)   the practice of any profession or the carrying on of any occupation, trade or business or employment in any job; or

(iv)   The use of, or access to any river, stream, spring, well, tank, cistern, water-tap or other watering place or any bathing ghat, burial or cremation ground, any sanitary convenience, any road, or passage, or any other place of public resort which other members of the public, or any section thereof, have a right to use or have access to; or

(v) the use of, or access to, any place used for a charitable or a public purpose maintained wholly or partly out of State funds or dedicated to the use of the general public or any section thereof ; or

(vi) the enjoyment of any benefit under a charitable trust created for the benefit of the general public or of any section thereof; or

(vii) the use of, or access to, any public conveyance; or

(viii) the construction, acquisition or occupation of any residential premises in any locality, whatsoever; or

(ix)   the use of any dharmshala, sarai or musafirkhana which is open to the general public, or to any section thereof; or

(x) the observance of any social or religious custom, usage or ceremony or taking part in, or taking out, any religious, social or cultural procession; or

(xi) the use of jewelry and finery;

shall be punishable with imprisonment for a term of not less than one month and not more than six months and also with fine which shall be not less than one hundred rupees and not more than five hundred rupees

Explanation- For the purposes of this section, "enforcement of any disability" includes any discrimination on the ground of "untouchability"

5. Punishment for refusing to admit person to hospitals etc.

Whoever on the ground of "untouchability"-

(a) refuses admission to any person to any hospital dispensary, educational institution or any hostel, if such hospital, dispensary, educational institution or hostel is established or maintained for the benefit of the general public or any section thereof; or

(b) does any act which discriminates against any such person after admission to any of the aforesaid institution;

shall be punishable with imprisonment for a term of not less than one month and not more than six months and also with fine which shall be not less than one hundred rupees and not more than five hundred rupees

6. Punishment for refusing to sell goods or render services

Whoever on the ground of "untouchability" refuses to sell any goods or refuses to render any service to any person at the same time and place and on the same terms and conditions at or on which such goods are sold or services are rendered to other persons in the ordinary course of business shall be punishable with imprisonment for a term of not less than one month and not more than six months and also with fine which shall be not less than one hundred rupees and not more than five hundred rupees.

7. Punishment for other offences arising out of "untouchability"

(1)   Whoever-

(a) prevents any person from exercising any right accruing to him by reason of the abolition of " untouchability" under article 17 of the Constitution; or

(b) molests, injures, annoys, obstructs or causes or attempts to cause obstruction to any person in the exercise of any such right or molests, injures, annoys or boycotts any person by reason of his having exercised any such right; or

(c)   by words, either spoken or written, or by signs or by visible representations or otherwise, incites or encourages any person or class of persons or the public generally to practice "untouchability" in any form whatsoever; or

(d)   insults or attempts to insult, on the ground of "untouchability" a member of a Scheduled Caste,

shall be punishable with imprisonment for a term of not less than one month and not more than six months, and also with fine which shall be not less than one hundred rupees and not more than five hundred rupees

Explanation-I   A person shall be deemed to boycott another person who-

(a)refuses to let to such other person or refuses to permit such other person, to use or occupy any house or land or refuses to deal with, work for hire for, or do business with, such other person or to render to him or receive from him any customary service, or refuses to do any of the said things on the terms on which such things would be commonly done in the ordinary course of business; or

(b)   abstains from such social, professional or business relations as he would ordinarily maintain with such other person.

Explanation-II.- For the purpose of clause (c) a person shall be deemed to incite or encourage the practice of "untouchability"-

(i) if he, directly or indirectly, preaches "untouchability" or its practice in any form; or

(ii) if he justifies, whether on historical, philosophical or religious grounds or on the ground of any tradition of the caste system or on any other ground, the practice of "untouchability" in any form.

(1A)   Whoever commits any offence against the person or property of any individual as a reprisal or revenge for his having exercised any right accruing to him by reason of the abolition of "untouchability" under article 17 of the constitution, shall, where the offence is punishable with imprisonment for a term exceeding two years, be punishable with imprisonment for a term which shall not be less than two years and also with fine.

(2)   Whoever-

(i)   denies to any person belonging to his community or any section thereof any right or privilege to which such person would be entitled as a member of such community or section, or

(ii)   takes any part in the ex-communication of such person, on the ground that such person has refused to practice "untouchability" or that such person has done any act in furtherance of the objects of this Act.

shall be punishable with imprisonment for a terms of not less than one month and not more than six months, and also with fine which shall be not less than one hundred rupees and not more than five hundred rupees

7A.(1)Whoever compels any person, on the ground of "untouchability" to do any scavenging or sweeping or to remove any carcass or to flay any animal or to remove the umbilical cord or to do any other job of a similar nature, shall be deemed to have enforced a disability arising out of "untouchability"

(2)Whoever is deemed under sub-section (1) to have enforced a disability arising out of "untouchability" shall be punishable with imprisonment for a term which shall not be less than three months and not more than six months and also with fine which shall not be less than one hundred rupees and not more than five hundred rupees.

Explanation- For the purposes of this section, "compulsion" includes a threat of social or economic boycott.

8.Cancellation or suspension of licences in certain cases

When a person who is convicted of an offence under section 6 holds any license under any law for the time being in force in respect of any profession, trade, calling or employment in relation to which the offence is committed, the court trying the offence may, without prejudice to any other penalty to which such person may be liable under that section, direct that the license shall stand cancelled or be suspended for such period as the court may deem fit, and every order of the court so canceling or suspending a license shall have effect as if it had been passed by the authority competent to cancel or suspend the license under any such law.

Explanation:- In this section, "lincence" includes a permit or a permission.

10. Abetment of offence

Whoever abets any offence under this Act shall be punishable with the punishment provided for the offence.

Explanation:- A public servant who willfully neglects the investigation of any offence punishable under this Act shall be deemed to have abetted an offence punishable under this Act.

THE SC AND ST PREVENTION OF ATROCITIES ACT 1989

In exercise of the powers conferred by sub-section (1) of Section 23 of the Scheduled Castes and the Scheduled Tribes (Prevention of Atrocities) Act, 1989 (33 of 1989), the Central Government hereby makes the following rules, namely:-

1.Short title and commencement. – (1) These rules may be called the Scheduled Castes and the Scheduled Tribes (Prevention of Atrocities) Rules, 1995.

(2) They shall come into force on the date of their publication in the Official Gazette.

2.Definitions:- In these rules, unless the context otherwise requires:-

(a)"Act" means the Scheduled Castes and the Scheduled Tribes (Prevention of Atrocities) Act, 1989 (33 of 1989);

(b)"dependent", with its grammatical variations and cognate expressions, includes wife, children, whether married or unmarried, dependent parents, widowed sister, widow and children of pre-deceased son of a victims of atrocity;

(c)"identified area" means such area where State Government has reason to believe that atrocity may take place or there is an apprehension of reoccurrence of an offence under the Act or an area prone to atrocity;

(d) "Non-Government Organisation" means a voluntary organisation engaged in the welfare activities relating to the scheduled castes and the scheduled tribes and registered under the Societies Registration Act, 1860 (21 of 1860) or under any law for the registration of documents or such organisation for the time being in force;

(e) "Schedule" means the Schedule annexed to these rules;

(f) "Section" means section of the Act;

(g) "State Government", in relation to a Union Territory, means the Administrator or the Union Territory appointed by the President under Article 239 of the Constitution;

(h) words and expressions used herein and not defined but defined in the Act shall have the meanings respectively assigned to them in the Act.

3. Precautionary and Preventive Measures.- (1) With a view to prevent atrocities on the Scheduled Castes and the Scheduled Tribes, the State Government shall:-

(i) identify the area where it has reason to believe that atrocity may take place or there is an apprehension of reoccurrence of an offence under the Act:

(ii) order the District Magistrate and Superintendent of Police or any other officer to visit the identified area and review the law and order situation;

(iii) if deem necessary, in the identified area cancel the arms licences of the persons,

not being member of the Scheduled Castes or Scheduled Tribes, their near relations, servants or employees and family friends and get such arms deposited in the Government Armoury;

(iv) seize all illegal fire arms and prohibit any illegal manufacture of fire arms:

(v) with a view to ensure the safety of person and property, if deem necessary, provide arms licences to the members of the Scheduled Castes and the Scheduled Tribes;

(vi) constitute a high power State-level committee, district and divisional level commi- ttees or such number of other committees as deem proper and necessary for assisting the Government in implementation of the provisions of the Act;

(vii) set-up a vigilance and monitoring committee to suggest effective measures to imp- lement the provisions of the Act;

(viii)set-up Awareness Centres and organise Workshops in the identified area or at some other place to educate the persons belonging to the Scheduled Castes and the Scheduled Tribes about their rights and the protection available to them under the provisions of various Central and State enactments or rules, regulations and schemes framed thereunder;

(ix)encourage Non-Government Organisations for establishing and maintaining Awareness Centres and organizing Workshops and provide them necessary financial and other sort of assistance;

(x)deploy special police force in the identified area;

(xi)by the end of every quarter, review the law and order situation, functioning of different committees, performance of Special Public Prosecutors, Investigating Officers and other Officers responsible for implementing the provisions of the Act and the cases registered under the Act.

4. SUPERVISION OF PROSECUTION AND SUBMISSION OF REPORT:-

(1)The State Government on the recommendation of the District Magistrate shall prepare for each District a panel of such number of eminent senior advocates who has been in practice for not less than seven years, as it may deem necessary for conducting cases in the Special Courts. Similarly, in consultation with the Director Prosecution/incharge of the prosecution, a panel of such number of Public Prosecutors as it may deem necessary for conducting cases in the Special Courts, shall also be specified. Both these panels shall be notified in the Official Gazette of the State and shall remain in force for a period of three years.

(2)The District Magistrate and the Director of Prosecution/in-charge of the prosecution shall review at least twice in a calendar year, in the month of January and July, the performance of Special Public Prosecutors so specified or appointed and submit a report to the State Government.

(3)If the State Government is satisfied or has reason to believe that a Special Public Prosecutor so appointed or specified has not conducted the case to the best of his ability and with due care and caution, his name may be, for reasons to be recorded in writing, denotified.

(4)The District Magistrate and the officer-in-charge of the prosecution at the District level,

shall review the position of cases registered under the Act and submit a monthly report on or before 20th day of each subsequent month to the

Director of Prosecution and the State Government. This report shall specify the actions taken/proposed to be taken in respect of investigation and prosecution of each case.

(5)Notwithstanding anything contained in sub-rule (1) the District Magistrate or the Sub- Divisional Magistrate may, if deem necessary or if so desired by the victims of atrocity engage an eminent Senior Advocate for conducting cases in the Special Courts on such payment of fee as he may consider appropriate

PERSONES WITH DISABILITY (EQUAL OPPORTUNITY, PROTECTION OF CIVIL RIGHTS) FULL PROTECTION ACT 1995.

CHAPTER I : PRELIMINARY

1. (1) This Act may be called the Persons With Disabilities (Equal Opportunities, Protection of Rights and Full Participation) Act, 1995.

(2) It extends to the whole of India except the State of Jammu and Kashmir.

(3) It shall come into force on such date as the Central Government may. by notification, appoint.

2. In this Act, unless the context otherwise requires,-

(a) "Appropriate Government" means,-

(i)In relation to the Central Government or any establishment wholly or substantially financed by that Government, or a Cantonment Board constituted under the Cantonment Act, 1924, the Central Government ;

(ii)In relation to a State Government or any establishment wholly or substantially financed by that Government, or any local authority., other than a Cantonment Board, the State Government;

(iii)In respect of the Central Co-ordination Committee and the Central Executive Committee, the Central Government;

(iv)In respect of the State Co-ordination Committee and the State Executive Committee, the State Government;

(b) "Blindness" refers to a condition where a person suffers from any of the following conditions, namely:-

(i)Total absence of sight. or

(ii)Visual acuity not exceeding 6160 or 201200 (snellen) in the better eye with correcting lenses; or

(iii)Limitation of the field of vision subtending an angle of 20 degree or worse;

(c)"Central Co-ordination Committee"   means   the   Central Co-ordination Committee constituted undersub-section (1) of section 3;

(d)"Central Executive Committee" means the Central Executive Committee constituted under sub- section (1) of section 9;

(e)"Cerebral palsy" means a group of non-progressive conditions of a person characterized by abnormal motor control posture resulting from brain insult or injuries occurring in the pre-natal, peri-

natal or infant period of development;

(f)"Chief Commissioner" means the Chief Commissioner appointed under subsection (1) of section

57;

(g)"Commissioner" means the Commissioner appointed under sub-section (1) of section 60;

(h)"Competent authority" means the authority appointed under section 50;

(i)"Disability" means-

(I) Blindness;

(ii)Low vision;

(iii)Leprosy-cured;

(iv)Hearing impairment;

(v)Loco motor disability;

(vi)Mental retardation;

(vii)Mental illness;

(j) "Employer" means,-

(i)In relation to a Government, the authority notified by the Head of the Department in this behalf or where no such authority is notified, the Head of the Department; and

(ii)In relation to an establishment, the chief executive officer of that the establishment;

(k)"Establishment" means a corporation established by or under a Central, Provincial or State Act, or an authority or a body owned or controlled or aided by the Government or a local authority or a Government company as defined in section 617 of 'the Companies Act, 1956 and includes Departments of a Government;

(l)"Hearing impairment" means loss of sixty decibels or more in the better year in the conversational range of' frequencies;

(m)"Institution for persons with disabilities" means an institution for the reception. Care, protection, education, training, rehabilitation or any other service of persons with disabilities;

(n)"Leprosy cured person" means any person who has been cured of leprosy but is suffering from-

(i)Loss of sensation in hands or feet as well as loss of sensation and paresis in the eye and eye-lid but with no manifest deformity;

(ii)Manifest deformity and paresis; but having sufficient mobility in their hands and feet to enable them to engage in normal economic activity;

(iii)Extreme physical deformity as well as advanced age which prevents him from undertaking any gainful occupation, and the expression "leprosy cured" shall be construed accordingly;

(o)"Loco motor disability" means disability of the bones, joints muscles leading to substantial restriction of the movement of the limbs or any form of cerebral palsy,

(p)"Medical authority" means any hospital or institution specified for the purposes of this Act by notification by the appropriate Government;

(q)"Mental illness" means any mental disorder other than mental retardation;

(r)"Mental retardation" means a condition of arrested or incomplete development of mind of a person which is specially characterized by sub normality of intelligence;

(s)"Notification" means a notification published in the, Official Gazette;

(t)"Person with disability" means a person suffering from not less than forty per cent. of any disability as certified by a medical authority;

(u)"Person with low vision" means a person with impairment of visual functioning even after treatment or standard refractive correction but who uses or is potentially capable of using vision for the planning or execution of a task with appropriate assistive device;

(v)"Prescribed" means prescribed by rules made under this Act;

(w)"Rehabilitation" refers to a process aimed at enabling persons with disabilities to reach and maintain their optimal physical, sensory, intellectual, psychiatric or social functional levels;

(x)"Special Employment Exchange" means any office or place established and maintained by the Government for the collection and furnishing of information, either by keeping of registers or otherwise, respecting-

(i)Persons who seek to engage employees from amongst the persons suffering from disabilities;

(ii)Persons with disability who seek employment;

(iii)Vacancies to which person with disability seeking employment may be appointed;

(y)"State Co-ordination Committee" means the State Co-ordination Committee constituted under sub- section (1) of section 19;

(z)"State Executive Committee" means the State Executive Committee constituted under sub-section

(l)of section 19

CHAPTER II : THE COORDINATION COMMITTEE

3. (1) The Central Government shall by notification constitute a body to be known as the Central Co-ordinationCommittee to exercise the powers conferred on, and to perform the functions assigned to it, under this Act.

(2) The Central Co-ordination Committee shall consist of-

(a)The Minister in charge of the Department of Welfare in the Central Government, Chairperson, ex officio;

(b)The Minister of State in-charge of the Department of Welfare in the Central Government, Vice- Chairperson, ex officio;

(c)Secretaries to the Government of India in-charge of the Departments of Welfare, Education, Woman and Child Development, Expenditure, Personnel, Training and Public Grievances, Health, Rural Development,

Industrial Development, Urban Affairs and Employment, Science and Technology. Legal Affairs, Public Enterprises, Members, ex officio;

(d)Chief Commissioner, Member, ex officio;

(e)Chairman Railway Board, Member, ex officio;

(f)Director-General of Lab our, Employment and Training, Member, ex officio;

(g)Director, National Council for Educational Research and Training, Member, ex officio;

(h)Three Members of Parliament. of whom two shall be elected by the House of the People and one by the Council of States, Members;

(I) Three persons to be nominated by the Central Government to represent the interests, which in the opinion of that Government ought to be represented, Members;

(j) Directors of the-

(I) National Institute for the Visually Handicapped, Dehradun;

(ii) National Institute for the Mentally Handicapped, Secundrabad;

(iii) National Institute for the Orthopaedically Handicapped, Calcutta;

(iv) Ali Yavar Jung National Institute for the Hearing Handicapped, Bombay,

Members, ex officio;

(k) Four Members to be nominated by the Central Government by rotation to represent the States and the Union territories in such manner as may be prescribed by the Central Government:

Provided that no appointment under this clause shall be made except on the recommendation of the State Government or, as the case may be, the Union territory;

(l) Five persons as far as practicable, being persons with disabilities. to represent non-governmentalOrganizations or associations which are concerned with disabilities, to be nominated by the Central Government, one from each area of disability, Members:

Provided that while nominating persons under this clause, the Central Government shall nominate at least one woman and one person belonging to Scheduled Castes or Scheduled Tribes;

UNIT V:

Poverty - illiteracy-unemployment-corruption- juvenile delinquency-alcoholism and drug addiction-commercial sex-AIDS-terrorism-environmental pollution.

POVERTY

It means state of lack for the basic needs

Two types

- Absolute poverty

"a condition characterized by severe deprivation of basic human needs, including food, safe drinking water, sanitation facilities, health, shelter, education and information."

- Relative poverty

"The term typically refers to inequality among individuals and groups within a society."

problems of poverty

- Hunger

- AIDS

- Pneumonia

- Diarrhea

- Tuberculosis

- Malaria

- Measles

Poverty alleviation programs in India

- Jawahar gram samridhi yojana (JGSY).

- National oldage pension (NAOP).

- National family benefit scheme (NFBS).

- Integrated rural development programe

- Rural housing indira awass yogana.

- MGNREGA 2005

Kumarasami kamaraj.

- Mid – day meal scheme.

- Major dam projects.

- Major Industries – NLC,BHEL.

ILLITERACY

Introduction

- In 1930 the U.S. Bureau of the Census defined as illiterate any person over ten years of age who was unable to read and write in any language.

- By the next census (1940) - the concept of "functional" illiteracy was adopted, and any person with less than five years of schooling was considered functionally illiterate, or unable to engage in social activities in which literacy is assumed.

- ? In 1970, the U.S. Office of Education considered at least six years of schooling (and sometimes as many as eight) to be the minimum criterion for functional literacy. In 1990 over 5% of the adult population living in the United States did not meet that criterion.

- Illiterate means unable to read and write.

- Adult literacy programs try to help people who somehow made it through the educational system without learning these basics. It can also mean not well-versed in a particular subject.

- If someone is a Science Fiction illiterate, they don't know or appreciate the genre.

- If someone is technologically illiterate, they probably need help sending email or accessing voice mail.

Literacy Rate in India

- ? Literacy is another proper indicator of economic development.

- ? A person in age limit of seven and above, who can both write and read with understanding in any of the language is considered as a literate in India.

- ? Population Census of India in 2001- 65.38%

- ? In 2011-74.04% Increase of 9 percent in the last 10 years

- ? It consists of male literacy rate 82.14% and female literacy rate is 65.46%.

- ? Kerala with 93.9% literacy rate is the top state in India.

- ? Lakshadweep - 92.3% and Mizoram -91.06% .

- Bihar with 63.08% literacy rate is the last in terms of literacy rate in India.

List of Steps taken by Government of India to improve Literacy Rate in India

- Free education programs to poor people living in villages and towns.

- Setting up of new school and colleges at district and state levels.

- Several committees have been formed to ensure proper utilization of funds allotted to improve literacy rate.

Ranking of States in India by Literacy Rate				
S.No	State	Literacy Rate (2011 Census)	Male Literacy Rate (2011 Census)	Female Literacy Rate (2011 Census)
1	Andaman & Nicobar Islands	86.3%	90.1%	81.8%
2	Andhra Pradesh	67.7%	75.6%	59.7%
3	Arunachal Pradesh	67.0%	73.7%	59.6%
4	Assam	73.2%	78.8%	67.3%
5	Bihar	63.8%	73.5%	53.3%
6	Chandigarh	86.4%	90.5%	81.4%
7	Chattisgarh	71.0%	81.5%	60.6%
8	Dadra & Nagar Haveli	77.7%	86.5%	65.9%
9	Daman & Diu	87.1%	91.5%	79.6%
10	Delhi	86.3%	91.0%	80.9%

- World Statistics institute (WSI), more than 27% people are illiterate globally.

- The main causes of this problem are social , motivational and family problems.

☐   Niger is the country having highest percentage of illiterate people. 84.3% people are not able to read, write or understand.

Illiteracy rate in world

☐   Almost three-quarters of the world's 775 million illiterate adults are found in only ten countries.

☐   In descending order: India, China, Pakistan, Bangladesh, Nigeria, Ethiopia, Egypt, Brazil, Indonesia, and the Democratic Republic of the Congo).

☐   Of all the illiterate adults in the world, two-thirds are women. Extremely low literacy rates are concentrated in three regions: South and West Asia and Sub-Saharan Sahelian Africa.

Malnutrition

- Definition

- Malnutrition is a group of conditions in children and adults generally related to poor quality or insufficient quantity of nutrient intake, absorption, or utilization.

- There are two major types of malnutrition:

- Protein-energy malnutrition - resulting from deficiencies in any or all nutrients

- Micronutrient deficiency diseases - resulting from a deficiency of specific micronutrients

Undernutrition

- Under nutrition is a consequence of consuming too few essential nutrients or using or excreting them more rapidly than they can be replaced.

- Infants, young children, and teenagers need additional nutrients. So do women who are pregnant or breastfeeding.

  Nutrient loss can be accelerated by diarrhea, excessive sweating, heavy bleeding (hemorrhage), or kidney failure. Nutrient intake can be restricted by age-related illnesses and conditions, excessive dieting, food allergies, severe injury, serious illness, a lengthy hospitalization, or substance abuse.

- The leading cause of death in children in developing countries is protein-energy malnutrition.

- Two types of protein-energy malnutrition have been described —kwashiorkor and marasmus. Kwashiorkor occurs with fair or adequate calorie intake but inadequate protein intake, while marasmus occurs when the diet is inadequate in both calories and protein.

- About 1% of children in the United States suffer from chronic malnutrition, in comparison to 50% of children in southeast Asia. About two-thirds of all the malnourished children in the world are in Asia, with another one-fourth in Africa.

Overnutrition

- Overnutrition results from eating too much, eating too many of the wrong things, not exercising enough, or taking too many vitamins or other dietary replacements.

- Risk of overnutrition is also increased by being more than 20% overweight, consuming a diet high in fat and salt, and taking high doses of:

- Nicotinic acid (niacin) to lower elevated cholesterol levels

- Vitamin A to clear up skin problems

- Iron or other trace minerals not prescribed by a doctor.

- Nutritional disorders can affect any system in the body and the senses of sight, taste, and smell. They may also produce anxiety, changes in mood, and other psychiatric symptoms.

- Malnutrition begins with changes in nutrient levels in blood and tissues. Alterations in enzyme levels, tissue abnormalities, and organ malfunction may be followed by illness and death.

Causes

- People who are malnourished may be skinny or bloated. Their skin is pale, thick, dry, and bruises easily. Rashes and changes in pigmentation are common.

- Other symptoms of malnutrition include:

- anemia

- diarrhea

- disorientation

- night blindness

Diagnosis, Treatment

- Overall appearance, behavior, body-fat distribution, and organ function can alert a family physician, internist,

  or nutrition specialist to the presence of malnutrition.

- Normalizing nutritional status starts with a nutritional assessment. This process enables a clinical nutritionist or registered dietician to confirm the presence of malnutrition, assess the effects of the disorder, and formulate diets that will restore adequate nutrition.

Maladjustment

- Definition

- It describes a person, usually a child, who has been raised in a way that does not prepare them well for the demands of life, which often leads to problems with behaviour in the future:a residential school for disturbed and maladjusted children.

- Causes of Maladjustment:

- The five main causes of maladjusted behaviour of adolescent are as follows:

- (i) Family

- (ii) Personal causes

- (iii) School-related causes

- (iv) Teacher-related causes

- (v) Peer-group related causes

- social maladjustment is a serious disturbance that will require time and resources to insure a child is able to succeed in mainstream schooling or other social environments.

- Professional Treatment for Social Maladjustment in Children

- Parental Interventions at Home

UNEMPLOYMENT IN INDIA

DEFINATION:

Unemployment is the state in which a person is without work, available to work, and is currently seeking work.

It is a situation where there is non-availability of job for the persons.

Its an situation in which a person who is physically capable, mentally willing to work at existing wage rate does not find any job and is forced to remain unemployed.

INTRODUCTION:

It involves a waste of human resource and results in many social evils like theft, pick- pocketing, robbery, murder etc. It's a serious economic, social and political problem of the country. It's a cause as well as effect of poverty. The unemployment rate is used in economic studies. Rate is determined as the percentage of those in the labor force without jobs.

There are a variety of different causes of unemployment, and disagreement on which causes are most important. Different schools of economic thought suggest different policies to address unemployment. Monetarists for example, believe that controlling inflation to facilitate growth and investment is more important, and will lead to increased employment in the long run. Keynesians on the other hand emphasize the smoothing out of business cycles by manipulating aggregate demand. There is also disagreement on how exactly to measure unemployment.

CONCEPTS OF UNEMPLOYMENT

1. Usual Status Unemployment
2. Current Weekly Status Unemployment
3. Current Daily Status Unemployment

1) Usual Stauts Unemployment: It is meant to determine the Usual Activity Status- employed, unemployed or outside the labour force. The activity status is determined with referance to a longer period, say a year preceding to the time of survey. It is a person rate and indicates constant unemployment.

2) Current Weekly Status: This concept determines activity status of a person with reference to a period of preceding seven days. In this period, if a person seeking job fails to get work for even one hour on any day, he is deemed to be unemployed.

3) Current Daily Status: This concept considers the activity status of a person for each person for each day of the preceding seven days .If he works for one day but less than four hours, then he is considered as employed for half a day.

Out of these concepts of unemployment, Current Daily Status concept provides most appropriate measure of unemployment.

UNEMPLOYMENT IN INDIA:

India as a nation is faced with massive problem of unemployment. Unemployment can be defined as a state of worklessness for a man fit and willing to work. It is a condition of involuntary and not voluntary idleness. Some features of unemployment have been identified as follows:

1. The incidence of unemployment is much higher in urban areas than in rural areas.
2. Unemployment rates for women are higher than those for men.

3. The incidence of unemployment among the educated is much higher than the overall unemployment.

4. There is greater unemployment in agricultural sector than in industrial and other major sectors.

TYPES OF UNEMPLOYMENT

Economists and social thinkers have classified unemployment into various types. Generally unemployment can be classified in two types:

🔲 **VOLUNTARY UNEMPLOYMENT:**

In this type of unemployment a person is out of job of his own desire doesn't work on the prevalent or prescribed wages. Either he wants higher wages or doesn't want to work at all. It is in fact social problem leading to social disorganization. Social problems and forces such as a revolution, a social upheaval, a class struggle, a financial or economic crisis a war between nations, mental illness, political corruption mounting unemployment and crime etc. threaten the smooth working of society. Social values are often regarded as the sustaining forces of society. They contribute to the strength and stability of social order. But due to rapid social change new values come up and some of the old values decline. At the same time, people are not is a position to reject the old completely and accept the new altogether. Here, conflict between the old and the new is the inevitable result which leads to the social disorganization in imposed situation. In economic terminology this situation is voluntary unemployment.

🔲 **INVOLUNTARY UNEMPLOYMENT:**

In this type of situation the person who is unemployed has no say in the matter. It means that a person is separated from remunerative work and devoid of wages although he is capable of earning his wages and is also anxious to earn them. Forms and types of unemployment according to Hock are.

a. **Cyclical unemployment** - This is the result of the trade cycle which is a part of the capitalist system. In such a system, there is greater unemployment and when there is depression a large number of people are rendered unemployed. Since such an economic crisis is the result of trade cycle, the unemployment is a part of it.

b. **Sudden unemployment** - When at the place where workers have been employed there is some change, a large number of persons are unemployed. It all happens in the industries, trades and business where people are employed for a job and suddenly when the job has ended they are asked to go.

c. **Unemployment caused by failure of Industries** - In many cases, a business a factory or an industry has to close down. There may be various factors responsible for it there may be dispute amongst the partners, the business may give huge loss or the business may not turn out to be useful and so on.

d. **Unemployment caused by deterioration in Industry and business** - In various industries, trades or business, sometimes, there is deterioration. This deterioration may be due to various factors. In efficiency of the employers, keen competitions less profit etc. are some of the factors responsible for deterioration in the industry and the business.

e. **Seasonal unemployment** - Certain industries and traders engage workers for a particular season. When the season has ended the workers are rendered unemployed. Sugar industry is an example of this type of seasonal unemployment.

Voluntary and Unvoluntary Unemployment (Graphically)
RURAL UNEMPLOYMENT:

This kind of employment prevails is on rural areas. The nature of problem is also complicated. There are only two types of unemployment commonly found in agricultural economy e.g. India

a) Seasonal Unemployment:

In an agrarian economy like India, seasonal unemployment is the most significant type of unemployment in rural sector. Agriculture labour in India is mostly dependent on monsoon.

b) Disguised Unemployment:

In the rural subsistence agrarian sector of the Indian economy, the problem of disguised unemployment is also typical. Disguised unemployment refers to that type of unemployment in which laborers appear to be working and employed but in reality, they are not employed as they do not add to the total output. In other words they are removed from their jobs, output would not decrease.

URBAN UNEMPLOYMENT:

This type of unemployment is found in urban areas i.e. towns and cities.

1) Industrial Unemployment:

This refers to unemployment amongst workers in industries and factories in urban areas. Industrial workers may be skilled or unskilled. Industrial is open unemployment.

2) Educated Unemployment:

It is the problem of educated middle class people of urban society. It means joblessness amongst the graduates, post graduates, doctors, engineers etc. However this type of unemployment does not exist in countries worldwide. These are specific type of unemployment that exist only in few countries especially those in involved in agricultural activities like India

CAUSES OF UNEMPLOYMENT

Unemployment levels are increasing dramatically in many parts of the world. There is considerable debate among economists as to the causes of unemployment. Keynesian economics emphasizes unemployment resulting from insufficient effective demand for goods and service in the economy. Others point to structural problems, inefficiencies, inherent in labour markets. Classical economics tends to reject these explanations, and focuses more on rigidities imposed on the labor market from the outside, such as minimum wage laws, taxes, and other regulations that may discourage the hiring of workers.

In the set up of a modern market economy, there are many factors, which contribute to unemployment.

Causes of unemployment are varied and it may be due to the following factors:

HIGH POPUALTION GROWTH:

The rapid increase in population of our country during the last decade has further worse the unemployment problem in the country. Due to rapidly increasing population of the country, a dangerous situation has arisen in which the magnitude of unemployment goes on increasing during each plan period.

JOBLESS GROWTH: Although India is a developing country, the rate of growth is inadequate to absorb the entire labour force in the country. The opportunities of employment are not sufficient to absorb the additions in the labour force of the country, which are taking place as result of the rapidly increasing unemployment in India.

INEFFICIENT AGRICULTURAL AND INDUSTRIAL SECTORS: Industrialization is not rapid in our country and industrial labor finds few job opportunities. As enough other employment opportunities are not available, agriculture is the principal area of employment in our country. Thus, pressure on land is high, as about 2/3 of the labor force is engaged in agriculture. Land is thus overcrowded and a large part of the work force is underemployed and suffer from disguised unemployment.

INAPROPRIATE EDUCATION SYSYTEM: After remaining at schools and colleges for a number of years men and women come out in large numbers, having gained neither occupational nor vocational training nor functional literacy from which all future skilled, educated professional, and managerial manpower is drawn.

WEAKNESSES IN PLANNING TECHNIQUES: The growth strategy underlying our plans has been found to be faulty. Lack in infrastructure development and poor labour-intensive techniques planning has made unemployment a severe issue in our Indian economy.

RECESSION
INFLATION

DISABILITY:

EFFECTS OF UNEMPLOYMENT

Unemployment has obvious and well-documented links to economic disadvantage and has also been connected in some discussion to higher crime rates especially among the young suicide, and homicide Garry Ottosen and Douglas Thompson (1996) broaden the consequences of unemployment, relating it to increases in the incidences of alcoholism, child abuse, family breakdown, psychiatric hospitalization, and a variety of physical complaints and illnesses. Some researchers have emphasized the importance of preventing youth from falling into unemployment traps. Robert Gitter and Markus Scheuer (1997) suggest that unemployment among youth not only causes current hardship, but may also hinder future economic success. This is because unemployed youths are not able to gain experience and on-the-job training and because a history of joblessness signals that the individual may not have the qualities that are valued in the labour market.

Attempts have, however, been made to estimate the economic cost associated with unemployment. Ottosen and Thompson (1996, p.5) noted that "the United States loses a little less than one percentage point of potential gross domestic product (GDP) or output for each one percentage point of unemployment. This implies that an unemployment rate of 7 percent costs the United States at least $400 billion annually in foregone output. This is more than $2,000 for every man, woman, and child over 16 years of age." Similarly, in Australia, Peter Kenyon (1998) calculated that the loss of GDP associated with an unemployment rate above the full-employment rate is the equivalent of one year's worth of GDP over the past two decades.

In addition to the loss of GDP, high unemployment increases the burden on social welfare programs. These include unemployment insurance programs and other types of welfare, such as food stamps, Medicaid, Medicare, and Supplemental Security Income (Ottosen and Thompson 1996). There are also intergenerational effects, as unemployment of parents will limit their capacity to finance the schooling of their children. As education is the primary means of social mobility, this intergenerational effect will give rise to an inheritance of inequality.

⬜   NATURAL RATE:

The natural rate of unemployment is the rate of unemployment where the labour market is in a position of equilibrium. This means that the labour supply = labour demand at a given real wage rate. All those people willing and able to take paid employment at the going wage rate do so.

The diagram below shows the labour supply (those willing and able to take work at a going wage rate) and the labour force - the number of active participants in the labour market. The labour force expands as the real wage rises because there is a greater incentive to search for paid work and sacrifice leisure.

Employment on the x-axis measures the total labour hours supplied by workers in the economy in a given time period. As the real wage increases, the total number of hours supplied by the labour force will expand.

The natural rate of unemployment is not zero - at the equilibrium wage W1 in the diagram above, there is unemployment measured by AB. This is made up of frictional plus structural unemployment. At a wage rate W2 (above the equilibrium "market-clearing wage") employment contracts along the labour demand curve and total unemployment rises (see the diagram below)

Dis-equilibrium unemployment rises to the level shown by the distance CD. This is because labour demand has fallen and the labour force has expanded. There is an excess supply of labour - some people who are willing and able to find employment cannot get paid work.

CORRUPTION IN INDIA

Definition

- ? **Corruption** means the state of being dishonest, especially in matters concerning money.

- ? It creates a very impact to the country's education, occupation, living style and mostly the humanity.

- ? India was ranked 94 out of 176 countries surveyed in the Corruption Perceptions Index (CPI) 2012,

Type

- ? On the basis of administration:-

- Political Corruption

- Administrative Corruption

- Professional Corruption

Causes

- Lack of employment

- Lack of proper system

- Lack of economical stability

- Lack of love for country

- Lack of autonomy(political independence)

- Lack of effective management and organisation

- Lack of effective leadership

Cures

- Value education

- Responsible citizen

- Effective leadership and administration

- Media

- Transparency

- Legislation(strict act's)

- Declaration of wealth and assets

- ⬚ Loyalty and patriotism

- ⬚ Effective and regular vigilance

Top corruption scams in India

- ⬚ 2G Spectrum Scam

- ⬚ Commonwealth Games Scandal

- ⬚ IPO Scandal

- ⬚ Satyam Scandal

- ⬚ Bofors Scam

- ⬚ The Fodder Scam

- ⬚ The Hawala Scandal

Anti Corruption ACT

- ⬚ The Prevention of Corruption Act came into force in September 1988. It was an improvisation of the Act of 1947.

- ⬚ Thus if an offence against a public servant is proved in the court there will be imprisonment of not less than 6 months upto 5 years and also the person may be fined.

Summary

- ⬚ All these corruptions are due to the leaders of this country, as well as the citizens.

- ⬚ The leaders are promoting the citizen towards corruption by showing money.

- ⬚ The main cause of corruption is also modernization of life style

- ⬚ In modern society they don't think about the country and its future, due to which indirectly they are responsible for this.

     ⦾   All the politicians should realize what their main duty is.

     ⦾   Black money should be sealed by the government.

     ⦾   Youths should make a revolution against it.

     ⦾   Punishment should be given to all the corrupt person in India.

JUVENILE DELINQUENCY

WHAT IS JUVENILE DELINQUENCY

* Crime commited by children and adolescents under statutory age is called juvenile delinquency.

JUVENILE DELINQUENT

*A juvenile delinquent is one who is a minor with major problems.

*Any person between the age 7 to 8,who violates the law is considered as criminals.

DIFFERENT FORMS OF DELINQUENNT BEHAVIOUR

*Loitering

* Lofting

*Pick-Pocketing

*Stealing

*gambling

*Sexual offences like eve teasing etc.

CAUSES OF JUVENILE DELINQUENCY

*FAMILY

*PEER GROUP

*NEIGHBOURHOOD

*EDUCATIONAL CURRICULUM

HOW TO CONTROL JUVENILE DELINQUENCY

1. Accept the delinquents as a person in his own right & give affection & security.

2. Providing the child with a variety of experiences like music & dance, art & craft.

3. Watch for the sign of maladjustment.

4. Attempt to build up a stable system of moral and social values.

5. Encourage the child to talk about & admit the existence of anti-social tendencies.

Alcoholism and Drug addiction

ALCOHOLISM

Alcoholism, also called alcohol dependence or alcohol addiction, is a destructive pattern of alcohol use that includes tolerance to or withdrawal from the substance. Alcoholism is appropriately considered a disease rather than a weakness of character or chosen pattern of bad behavior. It costs more than $165 billion per year in lower productivity, early death, and costs for treatment.

Causes of Alcoholism

Alcohol goes directly into the bloodstream, physically affecting the whole body. Some illnesses and health problems caused by alcohol include

Hangovers

Weight gain

High blood pressure

Cancer

Liver disease

Alcohol poisoning

Heart or respiratory failure

Effects of alcoholism

- Family problems

- .Work difficulties .

- Crime .

- Social effects

- Other long-term effects of heavy alcohol use include loss of appetite, vitamin deficiencies, stomach ailments, sexual impotence, central nervous system damage, and memory loss.

Signs or symptoms of alcoholism

Signs that indicate a person is intoxicated include the smell of alcohol on their breath or skin, glazed or bloodshot eyes, the person being unusually passive or argumentative, and/or deterioration in the person's appearance or hygiene. Other physical symptoms of the state of being drunk include flushed skin. Cognitively, the person may experience decreased ability to pay attention and a propensity toward memory loss

DRUG ADDICTION

- Drug addiction, also called substance dependence or chemical dependency, is a disease that is characterized by a destructive pattern of drug abuse that leads to significant problems involving tolerance to or withdrawal from the substance, as well as other problems that use of the substance can cause for the sufferer, either socially or in terms of their work or school performance. More than 2.6% of people suffer from drug addiction at some time in their life.

Causes of Drugs addiction

High doses of many of the drugs, or impure or more dangerous substitutes for these drugs, can cause immediate life-threatening health problems such as heart attack, respiratory failure, and coma. Combining drugs with each other or with alcohol is especially dangerous.

Cocaine

LSD

PCP

Stimulants

The Effects of Drug Addiction

Drug addiction, regardless of the types of drug used, has social, psychological and physical effects, such as:

- Health

- Society

- Family and relationship

- Changes in the structure and function of your brain from drug abuse make it impossible to safely stop using without professional intervention..

- Physical effects of drug addiction, heart attacks; breathing difficulties and respiratory arrest; nausea, vomiting, and abdominal pain; poor musculoskeletal development, cramping and muscle weakness; kidney and liver damage; seizures and memory loss; and cancer.

- Social effects are often noticed by family and friends of someone addicted to drugs. If you recognize a change in aggressiveness, selfishness, lying or a lack of interest in usual activities, you may be observing or experiencing the results of drug addiction.

Treatment for drug addiction

The treatment of dual diagnosis seems to be less effective when treatment of the individual's mental illness is separate from the treatment of his or her chemical dependency. More successful are integrated treatment programs that include interventions for both disorders. Such interventions are all the more improved by the inclusion of assessment, intensive case management, motivational interventions, behavior interventions, family treatment as well as services for housing, rehabilitation, and meditation treatment.

Sexual Health & Commercial Sex Workers
Definition of CSW Terms

- Varies from context to context but in the MOST general and BROAD sense it relates to:

"female, male and transgender adults and young people who receive money or goods in   exchange for sexual services, either regularly or occasionally, and who may or may not consciously define those activities as income-generating."

- The term *sex worker* has gained popularity over *prostitute* As those involved feel that it is less stigmatizing and say that the reference to work better describes their experience.

- But often associated with only females....problematic.

Background of Sex Work

- From historical times to present times CSWs have existed: this is not a 'modern phenomenon'!

- Their very existence in society indicates they serve a function (simple supply-demand).

- But are a highly stigmatised group-challenging basic family and sexual morality.

- Have been relegated to the margins of society, abused ,exploited & rights restricted as Citizens.

- HIV/AIDS-targeted as vectors of disease & clients as unwitting victims.

- CSWs tangled in webs of Stigma, shame and legality have been often left untouched in HIV programming

Types of sex work

- Formal (organized) or informal'(not organized).

- Formal sex work is establishment-based and managers and/or pimps act as clearly defined authorities and as intermediaries between the sex worker and client. Often found in Asia (brothels , bars, masseuse parlours)

- Informal sex workers, such as streetwalkers and self-employed call-girls or -boys, usually find their clients independently

- Occasional sex workers perform another type of informal sex work. They may sell or trade sex to meet short-term economic needs (e.g. school tuition, a family financial crisis). This type of sex work predominates in most African settings, where sex work is less likely to be a full-time occupation

Vulnerability of CSWs In the Context of Sexual Health

- Stigmatization and marginalization

- limited economic options, in particular for women

- limited access to health, social and legal services

- limited access to information and prevention means

- Gender-related differences and inequalities (Bargaining dynamics)

- Sexual exploitation and trafficking

- Harmful, or a lack of protective, legislation and policies

Exposure to risks associated with lifestyle (e.g. violence, substance use, mobility)

TERRORISM

What is terrorism?

- The world is deeply divided over what actions qualify as terrorism.
- **Terrorism is an instrument of political violence for a variety of ends.**
- **The State Department defines it as**
- **"premeditated, politically motivated violence perpetrated against noncombatant targets . . . usually intended to influence an audience."**
- **Terrorism is not an ideology!**

Who is a terrorist?

- The world is deeply divided over who is a terrorist.
- **Often the UN cannot resolve a debate over who is a terrorist and what is terrorism.**
- **There will always be those who will claim that some acts of violence against states**
- **and civilians are justified.**
- **That is, that another man's terrorist is their freedom fighter.**
- **There will always be those who claim that there is a universal standard for defining terrorism – and that the UN should act on the principle that, "one man's terrorist is another man's terrorist."**
- **Generally terrorist organizations are non-state actors.**
- **Some states legitimately support movements and causes that use terrorist methods.**

State sponsored terrorism:

- **through funding,**
- **safe haven,**
- **weapons and logistics.**

The US State Department continues to list the governments of Iran, Cuba, Iraq, Libya, Sudan, Syria, and (until recently) North Korea as state sponsors of terrorism.

Some states seek to use counterterrorism to win political leverage, and defeat their enemies by labeling them as "terrorists."
The UN cannot act effectively against terrorism,

since there is no international consensus on action.

Various groups described as terrorist:

South America:

- FARC (Colombia)
- The Shining Path or Sendero Luminoso (Peru)
- Tupac Amaru (Peru)

Africa

- The Shabab (Somalia)
- Armed Islamic Group (GIA in Algeria)

Middle East:

- Hizbollah (Lebanon)
- Hamas (Palestinian territories)

South Asia:

Sikh terrorism (India)

Europe:

October First Anti-Fascist Resistance Group (GRAP), a radical Marxist group (Spain)

Central Asia:

Al-Qaeda (operating out of Pakistan, Afghanistan, Sudan)

The Kurdish Workers Party (PKK)

North America:

Christian religious groups, such as the Aryan Nations.

The Jewish Defense League maintains a presence in North America as well.

What do terrorist organizations fight for?

Political autonomy/Separatism (the Basques, the PKK, ETA, in Kashmir, the Bodo tribes in Assam, Uigher in China, Chechens in Russia, Sikh militants fighting for an independent state of Khalistan).

Ideology (left-wing groups such as as the Turkish Revolutionary People's Liberation Party - Front (DHKP-C), the Peruvian Sendero Luminoso (Shining Path), and the Naxalites of India); NATO and American foreign policy (17th November, Greece)

Religious differences: Factional rivalry between Sunni and Shia Muslim Groups (in Pakistan)

Spillover: of the Algerian strife (France)

Creation of an Islamic state (al-Qaeda of Iraq, the Shabab in Somali, Algerian Armed Islamic Group (GIA), Creation of a Caliphate: al-Qaeda

Resistance of an occupation (Hamas + the Palestine Islamic Jihad)

Who or What is being targeted?

This different response can take the form of

1. attacks on civilians,

random attacks on tourists (recent terrorist attacks in Bali) and the deliberate killing of foreign-aid and NGO workers; incidents of kidnapping and hostage-taking have become frequent occurrences in South America and the former Soviet Union.

hoaxes, particularly bomb threats, have been employed on occasion to seriously disrupt transportation and tourism, causing significant local impact;

2. government facilities,

3. key economic targets ((such as those related to energy distribution, transportation, banking and tourism).

4. information systems.

Which methods do terrorist use?

At the lowest levels of conflict, attackers use such new forms of war as "cyberterrorism."

- the Internet is becoming a resource more frequently used by terrorists as a means to access information,
- spread propaganda,
- raise funds,
- communicate,
- and plan operations.

At the highest level of conflict, states, terrorist groups, or individuals can try to overcome an opponent's conventional military capabilities by using biological or nuclear weapons.

One of the first uses of a chemical nerve agent in a sarin terrorist attack, by the Aum Shinri Kyo cult in Tokyo in 1995, has been widely viewed as the crossing of a threshold (12 dead and 5,500 injured),

There have also been some limited attacks on nuclear power facilities worldwide; numerous unsubstantiated threats to trigger a nuclear explosive device;

and at least one reported case of the use of radiological materials—albeit in a very limited manner (the placing of a cesium capsule by Chechen rebels in a Moscow park)—by terrorists.

Increasingly sophisticated and willing travelers.

They have access to excellent false documentation and international contacts,

and can blend easily into a local émigré community, where they can plan and execute attacks without being readily identified.

How old is international terrorism?

About 40 years.

1968: three members of the Popular Front for the Liberation of Palestine (PFLP) hijacked an El Al Boeing 707, en route from Rome to Tel Aviv, carrying ten crew and 38 passengers.

What causes terrorism?

1. Public despair and humiliation are often fertile ground for terror organizers to exploit.

This is If this demand side persists, the terrorism phenomenon is unlikely to be contained.

For every terror organization that is destroyed, other suppliers will arise to exploit the persistent demand.

Bin-Laden, once he needed to rally public opinion in the region in the aftermath of 9/11, did not employ his grand political objectives for mobilizing political support.

Instead he highlighted issue that resonate with the public and that explain more fully the sense of despair and humiliation among Arabs and Muslims:

the Arab-Israeli issue and

sanctions against Iraq.

2. Terrorism thrives in anarchy: the weaker the central authority, the more numerous the militant groups and the more difficult it is to deter such groups, as one does not know whom to punish.

Not Syria but Lebanon,

Afghanistan,

Somalia,

Iraq.

Religion's role is not the central issue in understanding the terror phenomenon. This is not to say that religion plays no role, or that many Islamist groups are not dangerous or hostile.

When the violence in the Middle East was carried out by secular nationalists in the 1950s and 1960s, both the West and intellectuals in the region saw Islam as a passive religion that accepted the status quo and bolstered stability.

During that period the US and the West viewed secular national movements in the Middle East as the primary destabilizing political force in the region and viewed Islamic groups, especially those supported by friendly government, as more desirable and more stabilizing.

Religion and suicide bombers: the central reason motivating people to act, and to be recruited by violent groups, are hopelessness and humiliation, which have to do with expectations and interpretations of social and political relations.

Bin Laden's own recruitment tapes show that his primary means of motivating his supporter is to show the picture of dead Muslim in Palestine, Iraq, and Chechnya.

A transition from secular to religious:

Afghanistan (Mujahadeen, devoted to Islam and committed to Jihad ("Holy War"))

Algeria, Indonesia, Saudi Arabi, Tunisia, the Philippines, Chechnya, Kosovo, Bosnia, Iraq)

What has the US done to deal with terrorism? (Who is the US targeting?)

Afghanistan

Iraq

Shortly after the Sept. 11 attacks, Bush issued a classified order authorizing the C.I.A. to kill or capture Qaeda militants around the globe.

By 2003, American intelligence agencies and the military had developed a much deeper understanding of Al Qaeda's extensive global network,

Rumsfeld pressed hard to unleash the military's firepower against militants outside the combat zones of Iraq and Afghanistan.

(According to the report declassified in Nov. 2008) The United States military since 2004 has used secret authority to carry out nearly a dozen previously undisclosed attacks against Al Qaeda and other militants in Syria, Pakistan and elsewhere.

The 2004 order identified 15 to 20 countries, including Syria, Pakistan, Yemen, Saudi Arabia and several other Persian Gulf states, where Qaeda militants were believed to be operating or to have sought sanctuary.

These military raids were carried out by Special Operations forces (authorized by Rumsfeld and with the approval of President Bush). Some of the military missions have been conducted in close coordination with the C.I.A.

Examples:

1. In 2006, a Navy Seal team raided a suspected militants' compound in the Bajaur region of Pakistan.

(Officials watched the entire mission — captured by the video camera of a remotely piloted Predator aircraft — in real time in the C.I.A.'s Counterterrorist Center at the agency's headquarters in Virginia 7,000 miles away.)

The secret order gave the military new authority to attack the Qaeda terrorist network anywhere in the world, and a more sweeping mandate to conduct operations in countries not at war with the United States.

2. The Special Operations raid in Syria on Oct. 26, 2008.

3. Shortly after Ethiopian troops crossed into Somalia in late 2006 to dislodge an Islamist regime in Mogadishu, the Pentagon's Joint Special Operations Command quietly sent operatives and AC-130 gunships to an airstrip near the Ethiopian town of Dire Dawa. From there, members of a classified unit called Task Force 88 crossed repeatedly into Somalia to hunt senior members of a Qaeda cell believed to be responsible for the 1998 American Embassy bombings in Kenya and Tanzania.

But as many as a dozen additional operations have been canceled in the past four years, often to the dismay of military commanders.

Senior administration officials had decided in these cases that the missions were too risky, were too diplomatically explosive or relied on insufficient evidence.

Much of the world sees the US war on terrorism as being limited to a military campaign against suppliers without investing in the necessary political and economic instruments to reduce the central demand side.

ENVIRONMENTEL POLLUTION

"Environmental pollution is the biggest menace to the human race on this planet today. It means adding impurity to environment. The environment consists of earth, water, air, plants and animals. If we pollute them, then the existence of man and nature will be hampered."

AIR POLLUTION

- Pure air is always needed for inhaling.

- If we take pure air, our health improves.

- On the other hand impure air causes diseases and   impairs our health and causes our death.

- Smoke pollutes the air. It is the root of air pollution. The

smoke which is discharged from

1. Industries,

2. Automobiles and

3. Kitchens (is the mixture of carbon monoxide, carbon dioxide, methane etc. These are all poisonous gases).

- These cause lung-cancer, tuberculosis etc. which take a heavy toll of life.

- The glaring incident is the Bhopal gas leak in December 1984. Thousands of the residents of Bhopal died due to lungs problem which was caused by methylamine gas from the Union Carbide Plant.

NOISE POLLUTION

- The harsh sounds of buses, its, mopeds etc. affect our power of hearing and causes fart trouble. Is known as the sound pollution.

- It has been reported that there are two villages named Biraspalli and Devadas Palli near Dum Dum airport m Calcutta where a large number of people have lost their power of hearing. This is because of the frequent sounds of planes coming in and going out of Dum Dum Airport. The evils of sound pollution can be imagined from this example.

WATR POLLUTION

- The water of rivers and seas is being constantly polluted all over the world by various dangerous chemical and biological wastes.

- Mills and factories discharge very harmful waste waters into many rivers and sea.

- The water of the Ganges flowing by the side of both Varanasi and Calcutta is extremely polluted and contains all sorts of dangerous bacteria. It is really very strange and laughable that large number of the Indians regard this water as holy.

- They even drink this water for salvation. There is no doubt that the fish that grow in such waters are poisonous too.

CONTROL MEASURES

- It is more profitable to prevent pollution rather than deal with it after it has spread. To stop pollution before it is caused is the best course. Hence continuous modernization is equipment of environment management in also important.

- Where there is awareness among the people, the pressure on the government to control pollution is more. Even here, it is difficult to change the situation overnight.

- In order to address the problem before it arises, adoption of preventive measures is required. Whenever a developmental project is taken up, the proposed pollution control measures need to be incorporated into the environment impact assessment reports.

- Any developmental activity is bound to cause some damage to the environment. So the public must be informed about it before the work is taken up. The developmental projects must be strictly implemented as per the agreed environmental management terms.

- Under the environment Act, the state and central governments have developed an implementation mechanism with the help of the state and central pollution control Boards and the forest Department. The salient points to tackle environmental pollution at the community level are as follows-

- 1)From early childhood, children need to be taught about public health and sanitation, about citizens' right and duties towards natural resources. They should be encouraged to participate in activities addressing these issues.

- 2) The people in an area must learn to measure and estimate the amount of pollution in the surroundings, and at their own expense. Only then will determination and dedication to preserve the environment will arise. For this must be trained and helped the local pollution control board officials.

- 3)Every department of the government that supervises activities, which are likely of affect the environment and public health, should collect details on the effect of their activities on the public health, the environmental conditions, and the effects of pollution on various life forms. The departmental role in improving the environment must be clearly specified in every sector. Based on these details, the departments should develop and implement programs.

- 4)Where pollution is severe, the authorities should conduct continuous inspections, move out polluting industries or encourage them to modernize with latest technology. The region between industries and residential areas should be covered with thick green belt.

- 5)To prevent migration from villages to cities, small cities and towns should be developed with clear foresight and commitment. Healthy living conditions need to be provided in the villages protecting the lakes, trees and pastures. Zoning and town planning regulations pertaining to residential, commercial and industrial areas need to be made and the restrictions must be strictly enforced.

- 6)In cities and villages, solid waste is being thrown into the lakes. This mixes with the water and pollutes it. That is why waste needs to be separated into dry and wet wastes. The wet waste needs to be composted for agricultural use.

- 7)Domestic waste should kept separate from hospital and industrial wastes.

- 8)The wet waste from the cities should be turned into compost and must be retuned to the farms through agricultural markets, Rythu bazaars and with the help of market committees.

- 9)Environmental protection is a joint effort. That is why universities, scientific institutions, governmental organizations, and colleges need to work together. They should test the purity of air, water and land in their areas. Special attention should be paid to biodiversity in the area.

- 16)Cleaner raw materials must be used and cleaner production processes need to be followed and encouraged. Pollution during the process of production should be reduced production must be carried on generating minimum wastes.

Even after the end of live of a product or material, it should not damage the environment around us. We must encourage the production of such materials.

•   17)To reduce air pollution in our cities, we must reduce vehicular pollution. This can be achieved only through an efficient railway system.

•   18)Sewage water needs to be treated and used or irrigation. It should not be allowed to enter into water bodies.

•   19)Drinking water, storm water and sewage are getting mixed up in our villages and cities. We should stop this and divert the used water away from the drini9ng water sources.

•   20)Every farmer needs to be encouraged to construct a small farm pond in the field to store rainwater and to use it for agriculture. Synthetic chemical pesticides and fertilizers are entering the rivers and lakes and polluting them. These contaminants are entering the food chain. We need to replace synthetic chemical fertilizers and pesticides with organic fertilizers and pesticides to protect our food from contamination

"AS AN HUMAN ITS OUR RESPONSIBILITY TO SAVE RESOURSES FOR OUR FUTURE GENERATION SO THINK WEATHER OUR ACTION IS NOT EFFECTING NATURE AND FUTURE AND SAVE THE RESOURCE"

CONTACT	
CREATOR	T.M.SURESH
ABOUT PROJECT MSW	CONVERSION OF SOCIAL WORK STUDY MATERIALS (IN PAPER) INTO SOFT COPIES, ELIMINATING THE DIFFUCILTIES IN GETTING STUDY MATERIALS.
WANT TO JOIN PROJECT MSW	EMAIL US TO mailto:tms3292@gmail.comtms3292@gmail.comOR CALL US AT 91-9626633799.